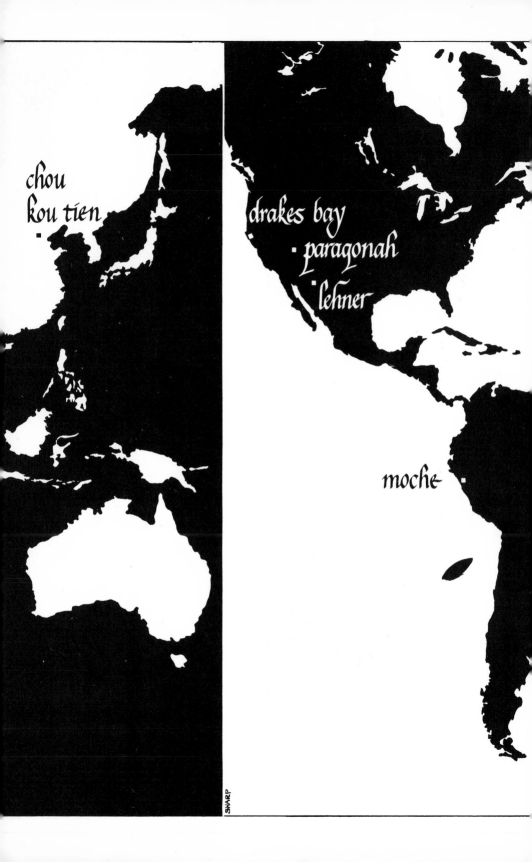

la colombière
sutton hoo
ur
tutankhamen's tomb
olduvai

SITES

Figure 1

ARCHAEOLOGY:

An Introduction

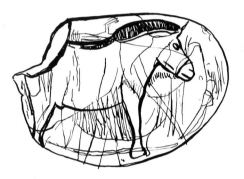

CHANDLER PUBLICATIONS IN

ANTHROPOLOGY *and* SOCIOLOGY

LEONARD BROOM, EDITOR

CHANDLER PUBLISHING COMPANY
124 Spear Street, San Francisco, California 94105

ARCHAEOLOGY

AN INTRODUCTION

By Clement W. Meighan

UNIVERSITY OF CALIFORNIA,
LOS ANGELES

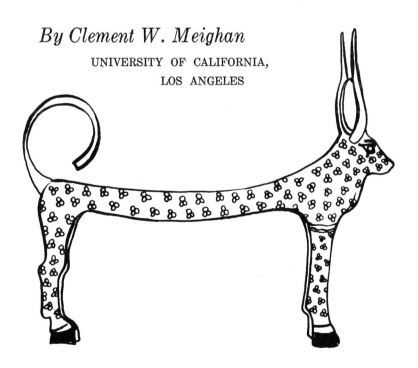

CONTENTS

ILLUSTRATIONS

Illustrations are identified as to source, when necessary, in the legends that accompany them. Illustrations not identified as to source are either from my own collection or from the files of the Department of Anthropology, University of California, Los Angeles.

TABLES

FOREWORD

This book aims to present the methods and point of view of the archaeologist in studying his material — what he thinks about, why he thinks the way he does, and how his thinking differs from the average museum visitor's. As with other studies, one's knowledge and appreciation can be much enhanced by viewing the subject through the eyes of the professional.

I have chosen to write about specific sites and discoveries as much as possible rather than to deal with generalities. Instead of discussing cultural levels in general (like "lower paleolithic"), I have instead examined individual explorations (like the cave at Chou Kou Tien) that exemplify the cultural remains of this level. This procedure may give the effect of a series of snapshots rather than a movie unfolding the great sweep of human development. Yet it shows the way archaeologists make deductions and demonstrates how we have learned what we know about human development. It also suggests the intellectual challenge and excitement of archaeological research.

Through examination of individual discoveries and what was inferred from them, it is possible to gain an understanding of archaeology as a search for new knowledge — a dynamic kind of scholarly exploration rather than a mere catalog of objects and dates.

xi

The approach via specific examples avoids some of the pitfalls of more conventional ways in which archaeological history is presented. For example, the most common summary begins with the simplest remains and moves straight to the complex civilizations of today. Although such a summary is compact, it gives the impression of a continuous and even advance in human knowledge and minimizes the various blind alleys, side developments, and marginal civilizations that may remain at a very simple stage even while great complexity is appearing elsewhere. Another way of summarizing archaeology is through an areal approach, and many excellent regional summaries are available. However, such a presentation can give the impression of a culture developing in isolation without contact with other cultures. For some areas of the world, notably the Near East, such an approach can become a tedious chronicle of kings and royal activities — a political rather than a cultural history.

The spectacular approach, in which every discovery is a magnificent temple, a tomb filled with golden idols, or some other find of intrinsic or artistic merit, is the most superficial possible view since it presents the archaeologist as primarily a treasure seeker. Another approach, naive and all too common, consists of treating a vast and complex cultural development as if it were all on one time level. This produces short treatises on such topics as "The Ancient Egyptians" which may compress 3,000 years of cultural history into a hopeless montage of cultural features, drawn from periods millenia apart.

The approach via specific examples facilitates discussing in some detail the objects found and the interpretations drawn from them. The examples in this book have been chosen to cover the broadest possible range, from very ancient times to recent periods, from extremely simple cultures to elaborate civilizations, from both the Old World and the New World. Two are from sites I have excavated myself; the remainder are from publications of other scholars as cited in the references at the end of each section.

I wrote this book for two reasons. One was a desire to communicate to the layman some of the things that an archaeologist does, to arouse in him some of the same curiosity and interest that made me an archaeologist. In addition, I thought I would enjoy dealing with archaeology in general rather than with the particularized research projects to which most of the archaeologist's time is devoted. Whether my first aim is successful or not, the second purpose has been amply fulfilled; I did enjoy myself and learned in the process. If the reader can do the same, the time was well spent.

ARCHAEOLOGY:

An Introduction

THE ARCHAEOLOGIST:
What He Studies and What He Does

Archaeology is a discipline that draws historical conclusions from objects — often from fragmentary objects. It is the scientific study of the material remains of man's past life and activities. Though these material remains may include written records, the archaeologist gives way to the historian as written records grow more numerous and thorough.

All archaeology is history, that branch of knowledge that records and explains past events. But not all history is archaeology; political history in particular is a kind to which the archaeologist can usually contribute little. The historian need not usually hold himself to reconstructing the past primarily from material remains but expects also to utilize oral and written records extensively. Indeed, professional historians tend to forgo using many of the archaeologists' resources. Some individual studies can be assigned as readily to history as to archaeology, but for the most part historians and archaeologists are people with different sorts of backgrounds, engaged in somewhat different approaches to the study of man's past. The archaeologist deals with the total span of human development, the ninety-nine per cent that is not written as well as the one per cent that is documented by written records. It is apparent that different sorts of historical record are derived in the one case from broken pottery, buried skeletons, and crumbled walls and in the

1

other case from a record which gives intimate written details of a conqueror or a vanquished people.

One basic feature of archaeological work is that no matter what the special study, it pertains in some way to the activities of man. It is not concerned with rocks, minerals, or fossils *unless* these things have some bearing on human activity. Archaeologists are students of human development, historians if you like, but scholars whose methods and results are somewhat different from those of historians because of their different sources of data.

Despite this central interest in human development, the research of individual archaeologists may have very diverse approaches. In actual practice, the archaeologist may be concerned at various times with fossil animals, the climate of the Pleistocene period, the marine life of a particular coast, the art of primitive people, or dozens of other special studies. At first glance, such diversity gives to archaeology the appearance of a chaotic and hodge-podge study.

The emphasis of a particular archaeological study is related to the kind of remains under consideration. Depending on what is available for study, the archaeologist's research will move in the direction of emphasizing the *natural sciences,* the *social sciences,* or the *humanities.*

For the earliest periods and the more simple cultures, archaeology is largely a natural science because primitive man lived much like the animals he hunted. Most of his time had to be spent in the search for food, leaving little for the development of a complex society, and even less for philosophy, art, religion, and the similar aspects of human life that are now classified as the humanities. The simpler cultures require approach in the light of their own view of life, heavily affected by the need to make a living with a simple technology, often in a hostile environment such as desert or arctic regions. Archaeological studies in this category are concerned with problems overlapping those of biology, geography, and ecology; that is, the archaeologist is primarily concerned with the areal distribution of the people and their relation to their environment.

As men developed their skills at coping with environmental problems, primarily by invention of better tools and weapons, they could secure food in greater abundance. The population increased, and the increase led to the need for the greater development of organized society. Within organized society there were often chiefs, kings, social classes, and specialists in different occupations. To study the activities of men in such cultures, the archaeologist has need for the data and concepts of the *social sciences*. Social development and social interaction may be the central concern of some archaeological studies, but the scholar interested only in these matters finds very little to study in the remains of the simpler communities where most of life was involved in the food quest.

The *humanities* become important to the archaeologist when he moves to the study of a society with a secure food supply and the consequent leisure time available for artistic and philosophic creativity. The humanities, which since the invention of writing have become more and more significant in human life, assume a large share of the archaeologist's time when he is studying civilizations like those of the ancient Near East, Egypt, and Greece.

The relative magnitude of the natural-science, social-science, and humanities areas of human activity is indicated in Fig. 2. During most of human history some part of all three areas has existed, and the thorough archaeologist is obliged to look for evidence of each. Yet the variety of man's ancient pasts causes one archaeologist to use much of his time in a style analysis of vase painting, another to identify and tabulate animal bones from an ancient village.

The variety of searches in archaeological work leads to a practical problem and to a positive intellectual value. The problem lies in the difficulty of classifying archaeology into one of the usual departments into which the college curriculum is divided. Few American universities have a department of archaeology. Instead, archaeology is taught in language departments (such as Near Eastern or Oriental languages), classics or humanities departments (usually concerned primarily with Greek and Roman aspects of archaeology), or in social-science departments, such as anthropology. In a few cases archaeology courses are taught in conjunction with the natural sciences under such headings as geology and paleontology. Most American archaeologists earn their academic degrees in anthropology, the least specialized of the disciplines mentioned; anthropological archaeologists readily develop special studies in any of the directions given above. Anthropology has a major advantage for archaeologists in its many detailed studies of primitive peoples of the world. Many of the things dug up by archaeologists are not recognizable without reference to the simpler

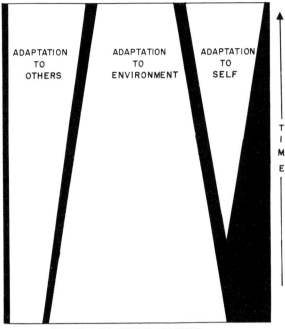

ADAPTATION
TO
OTHERS

ADAPTATION
TO
ENVIRONMENT

ADAPTATION
TO
SELF

T
I
M
E

TOTALITY OF HUMAN CULTURE

Fig. 2. Human adaptation through time. *At the very beginning of human existence, adaptation to environment occupies nearly all of man's attention, only a little of his culture being concerned with social factors and none with self-realization. Only when the external demands (of environment and adjustment to other people) have been met does the "inner man" get much attention. Archaeological remains reflect the relative proportions of these major adaptations for prehistoric peoples.*

peoples of the world who today make and use devices that have long since passed out of use in modern civilization. Archaeologists are forced to base their interpretation on things, and the interpretation is much aided when the things can be found still in use by someone, somewhere among the peoples of the world.

Despite the confusion over academic headings, diversity of studies proves to be in fact archaeology's greatest strength. Archaeology provides a meaningful bridge between the natural sciences, the social sciences, and the humanities, and in a broad understanding of archaeology there is an over-all view of man's place in the world that is difficult to attain by any other means. Archaeology, in spanning human history from the ultimate beginnings, in all areas and under all kinds of conditions, requires a breadth of understanding not accessible through the traditional compartmented academic subjects.

The three main academic divisions, artificial as they are, correspond rather closely to the three major needs of all individuals in all human groups: making a living (natural science), getting along with other people (social science), and satisfying the "inner man" through development of peace of mind (the humanities). These irreducible necessities of human life must be met through satisfactory adaptations if the individual or the society is to survive and flourish. This pattern of needs provides a useful frame of reference for viewing prehistoric societies — we can investigate a prehistoric community to discover how the people solved the problems of adaptation. Such understanding of prehistoric societies contributes to an understanding of the development of culture in general and also may enhance understanding of the particular adaptations that have led to modern society.

Table 1 relates archaeology to the basic adaptations which every person and society must make. The fact that man is an animal requires him to have a food supply, which in turn dictates that he develop some means of obtaining food from his environment. Failure to do so results in starvation and death.

There is also a biological basis for social organization. Man is raised in a family and social group because the human infant is helpless for a long period and must have adult help to survive, unlike other animals whose young can often survive on their own immediately after birth. The ordering of family and social groups, scarcely a need for many other animals, is a compelling need for man.

Finally, even the satisfaction of the "inner man" has a biological basis in the large brain and complex nervous system of the human organism as compared to other animals. Cats and dogs do not need art, philosophy, and explanations of the universe; humans seem driven to seek such things by the kind of brain they are born with.

The chart makes a distinction between the responses of individuals and the responses of groups to the common needs. Groups are made up of individuals and group responses therefore correspond to individual responses. The individual's response to his "awareness of self," for example, is to seek inner contentment or "peace of mind" — the group response is to try to provide these through education and other "social" activity. It is also important to note that a

TABLE 1. ARCHAEOLOGY AND THE BASIC ADAPTATIONS OF SOCIETIES AND INDIVIDUALS

	Biological basis	Responses	Possible results of failure to make adequate adaptation
I. ADAPTATION TO ENVIRONMENT (The *natural sciences* of strong concern in archaeology)	*Individual:* Man an animal	Obtain food and shelter	Starvation, death
	Society: Tendency of species to compete for existence with other organisms	Develop techniques of exploitation; technology, economics	Extinction
II. ADAPTATION TO OTHERS (The *social sciences* of significant concern in archaeology)	*Individual:* Raised in family setting	Make personal adjustments to others	Neurosis, crime, anti-social behavior
	Society: Long dependence of human infant on adults	Develop family and social organization, law, politics, religion and ritual	War, riot
III. ADAPTATION TO SELF (SATISFACTION OF THE "INNER MAN") (The *humanities* of significant concern in archaeology)	*Individual:* Large and complex brain, innate curiosity	Seek understanding, peace of mind	Neurosis, anxiety, various mental breakdowns
	Society: Stimulation of one intellect by another	Elaborate education, religion, philosophy, arts, and humanities	Destructive internal conflict; race riots, hypernationalism

failure on the part of the individual may destroy him but not destroy the group or society. Many individuals may starve but the food supply may be sufficient to insure continuance of the group. Yet societies too may disappear if the adaptation of the society as a whole is inadequate.

The table does not try to show the many choices open to individuals; it does intend to show the areas in which some adaptation is essential. It is essential to get food from the environment, but some individuals will hunt, some fish, some farm. Some groups will cope with a desert, others with arctic environments. Some choose to eat pork; some may make it taboo. None can choose whether or not to eat anything.

The significance of these categories for the archaeologist is as a checklist of areas of investigation in archaeological research. The needs of modern man include the needs of extinct man. Reconstruction of past life depends on the discovery and explanation of just what ancient man did to cope with these universal problems. Such a frame of reference also reminds us of the essential human qualities of ancient man. He was man, neither more animal nor more godlike than modern man; he faced the kind of major problems we face.

But the study of past societies is pursued in the presence of some inherent difficulties.

First, the limitations of archaeological data must be recognized. Most of the information comes from material objects lost, hidden, or discarded by former people. Since there is more to human life than the objects used by people, the reconstruction based on objects alone must of necessity be fragmentary. Many important aspects of living are not evidenced by imperishable objects that last for hundreds or thousands of years buried in the ground. Language is one such aspect; unless written documents have been left behind, it is impossible in most cases to have any idea of the language spoken by the prehistoric group. Likewise, the people's philosophy, their morals, their songs and stories are discernible only indirectly, if at all, in the material debris available for study.

A second basic fact of archaeology is that human remains become more abundant and diverse as time nears the present. The presence of the automobile in our culture has entailed a tremendous number of specialized tools and parts, for example; it is obvious that the culture of the present has both more material things and more *kinds* of things than ever before. And this example carries us back only to preautomobile times. The archaeologist can and does study groups that lived before there were metals, before books, before agriculture, and so back to a time when man had no durable object beyond a rudimentary bone club or chipped rock.

A third basic fact comprises chance. The difficulties of studying human development are greatly increased as one goes back in time, and indeed the study of the oldest human remains is so difficult that an element of luck enters in; many of the finds are accidental discoveries. The reasons are several; in the beginnings of culture there were few people, hence few tools to be left behind. Of this few, only a fraction have been preserved somehow against the effects of climate, floods, landslides, and other destructive forces which could obliterate them through thousands of years. Further, the tools were so crude that they may not be recognized as human manufactures. And finally, having survived the trials of time, the remains must be found, recognized for what they are, and described in print so that people can know about them. Considering these obstacles, it is not surprising that we know so little about our earliest forebears.

2 THE ARCHAEOLOGIST'S METHODS AND TOOLS

The archaeologist's work is done in the field and in the laboratory primarily. Of the two, the work in the field is more often publicized, especially the aspects that support reverie about romance, glamor, perhaps buried treasure, and travel. The fruitful and unspectacular work of laboratory analysis and description, the library and museum research, the historical scholarship, and the financing receive less frequent attention. This chapter deals with some aspects of field and laboratory work.

THE ARCHAEOLOGICAL EXPEDITION

While many archaeological expeditions consist of a group of students and their instructor who spend a week end investigating a site near their university, it is true that some expeditions are more imposing and expensive. A few words are in order about what the archaeologist and the would-be archaeologist do in the field expedition.

At the simplest level, the main requirements for archaeological field work are patience and the willingness to record carefully a multitude of more or less routine observations. An archaeological field party can often make use of volunteers who share the tasks of sorting endless potsherds, cataloging specimens, and exposing and recording finds uncovered in the course of the digging. However, tasks of this kind seldom justify the expense of transporting

9

an amateur worker to the project, let alone merit a salary. Many amateurs have paid their own transportation to an expedition camp and have contributed hundreds of hours of time to the vitally important but nonetheless tedious details of archaeological recording. If he does not attract such dedicated helpers and colleagues, however, the field archaeologist usually finds that he can train native or local labor to do much of the work, and that his expedition budget will go further if he employs local people instead of transporting his help hundreds or thousands of miles.

The average archaeological expedition is much smaller than the popular image suggests. Even when a crew of 40 or 50 laborers is used, the number of professional archaeologists is usually only one or two, and it practically never exceeds six to eight for a field project. Those chosen for staff positions must, therefore, have more to offer than willingness or patience. An archaeologist is a scholar who not only knows how to dig, but can exercise judgment about digging; he knows what is important and what not so important, when to dig fast and when to move with extreme caution, and when to abandon excavation in one area and move to another. This kind of "field sensitivity" can come only with practice and with the experience of translating field activities into written archaeological reports.

The archaeologist in charge of a new project tries to recruit for his staff people who not only have technical ability (in such skills as photography, surveying, and drafting) but who also have a "feel" for archaeology and can supervise various aspects of the digging. Personality is very important, not only in getting along with the other crew members under field conditions that are often uncomfortable and sometimes trying, but also in the indispensable tasks of working with local officials, foreign-government representatives, and crews of native labor.

The best advice that can be given to those who hope someday to accompany an archaeological dig to Egypt or Peru is to develop skills by working with small-scale projects close to home, and in such projects to prove themselves competent, careful workers who can be depended upon under field conditions. There are always plenty of volunteers for the "glamor" projects in archaeology, but those chosen are the ones who have already demonstrated their ability in smaller and more routine programs of field investigation.

A person who has a serious interest in archaeology should investigate before affiliating himself with amateur archaeology groups. Even college-level courses in field archaeology may be so inadequate as to be harmful to the serious student, if such courses are taught by persons who themselves have little or no training in archaeology. To appraise the value of an archaeological program, the prospective volunteer can find out whether the person in charge is competent by asking the following questions:

Has the field leader published articles in professional archaeological journals? Publication perhaps is the most important single test, since an archaeologist whose writings are accepted as professional by his colleagues has some knowledge of the subject. In the United States the foremost archaeological journals are *American Antiquity* (published by the Society for American Archaeology) and the *American Journal of Archaeology* (published by the Archaeological Institute of America). In addition, there are dozens of university series and regional journals publishing archaeological articles of scholarly quality.

It is also fair to ask if the academic background of the field leader includes formal study of archaeology. People who would hesitate to classify themselves as geologists, biologists, or chemists without having had any training in these studies often seem to have no compunctions about calling themselves archaeologists and even leading expeditions on the basis of having gone on a field trip or having read a couple of books about archaeology.

Finally, if the field leader has a large private collection of antiquities and if he is involved in buying and selling antiquities, his interest in archaeology may well be suspect. If the leader and his group collect for themselves or commercialize their work, then their scholarly motivations (and their ability to provide good training) are questionable.

Such guides are, of course, not infallible, but they are commonsense queries the novice can use to judge for himself if a given group is engaged in archaeological research or if the individuals are simply collecting objects of the past.

There are many legitimate and productive groups involved in archaeological exploration and research. There are few places (in the United States at least) where the would-be archaeologist cannot find a school or amateur group with which he can work. Several state archaeological societies have more than a thousand members with branches in several towns. For beginners, it is usually more profitable to work with an organized group, since guidance in field techniques will be available. Trying to do an excavation single-handed is seldom profitable because of the number of man-hours needed in most cases to obtain an adequate collection for study. Solo efforts may require months or even years of part-time digging before enough objects are recovered to merit analysis.

Yet it is not always possible for the interested amateur to affiliate himself with group archaeological projects, and for such persons the choice is between "do it yourself" archaeology and none at all. For individual workers a guide to field methods can be obtained by studying the works cited at the end of this chapter. One of these, *The Archaeologist's Note Book*, contains printed forms and explanations for recording basic field observations. Most professional archaeologists would be dismayed at the prospect of untrained individuals starting out to dig on their own, but for those who insist on doing field exploration, careful use of the published guides can yield results of modest value to archaeology rather than mere collections of meaningless objects.

A word of caution for the would-be digger: most countries have antiquities laws that forbid excavation except as licensed by authorities. Usually the national museum of the country can give information on requirements for a permit. The penalty for unauthorized digging can be severe, particularly where valuable objects are to be found, as in Mexico, Peru, and Egypt. In the United States, there is a national antiquities law (penalties can include confiscation of collection, six months in jail, and a $500 fine) ; in addition, most states have legal restrictions against unscientific digging. Not only in the scientific sense, but also legally, archaeology is not to be confused with treasure hunting.

THE PROCESS OF EXCAVATION

Though excavation may have any of several specific objectives, according to the area of the work and the interests of the individual scholar, the steps in any digging process are much the same:

First, a survey is made of the area to be studied, in order to locate the principal archaeological remains and to get an idea, from surface finds and an occasional test pit, of the variety of archaeological finds to be studied. The survey area may be a limited physiographic unit (an island or a river valley) or a whole region, state, or country. One might think that such preliminary work had already been accomplished for the whole world, but in fact most of the world has not yet had even preliminary surveys for archaeological remains.

Following the survey, one or more of the sites found is selected for intensive excavation. If the excavation is the first to be done in the area, the archaeologist often picks the largest or deepest site, with the hope of getting the maximum time-span and variety of remains for study.

Once the site is chosen, plans must be made for housing and maintaining a field crew at the location. This is often a major task, particularly where concessions must be obtained from a foreign government, equipment crated and shipped, and careful planning done to insure the key items of excavation equipment will be available when they are needed. For a large project, several months of planning are necessary before the crew begins the field work.

A careful contour map is made of the site area so that any find can be precisely located with respect to any other find or physical feature of the site. To map a small site may take half a day; several weeks may be needed to map a location in a jungle area with many mounds scattered over a square mile or more. In recent years aerial photography has been increasingly important for finding and mapping archaeological locations.

An early essential is the establishment of a *datum,* a point from which all measurements are made. Such a datum may be a permanent feature already present (like the corner of a concrete bridge culvert) or it may be installed by the archaeologists; the essential requirement is that it be a permanent measuring point for future reference.

As the digging proceeds, the appropriate techniques are dictated by the nature of the site and of the investigation. Archaeologists rarely dig everything in an ancient site; the usual digging samples only a very small part of the site remains. To be sure, once a pit is begun, the archaeologist tries to continue digging until he reaches a level without any cultural indications (sherds, charcoal, or other signs of human effort) but few excavators ever dig more than 10 per cent of the area of a site. Such sampling is usually dictated by practical considerations of time and cost — to excavate many of the larger sites in entirety would take years and hundreds of thousands of dollars. Besides, it is seldom necessary to dig a whole site to attain the goal of cultural reconstruction. The general rule is to dig until the pattern of finds becomes repetitive and little new information comes to light. For a small site representing the camp of a hunter-gatherer group, an adequate sample may require a few man-days; for a large and complex site of agriculturalists, thousands of man-days are usually necessary. The skillful archaeologist is one who can both select a good spot for excavation and judge when to *stop* digging and move on. This capacity marks a distinction between scholarly archaeology and mere collecting; the collector digs as long as he finds specimens, while the archaeologist stops when he has a complete enough record to permit cultural reconstruction.

Many books on "how to dig" are available. Some are listed, along with books on other aspects of method, at the end of this chapter.

METHODS AND INTERPRETATIONS

Much reconstruction of the life of past times takes place well after the discovery of remains or the actual digging process. But the process must be fitted to the basic kinds of information sought by the archaeologist. To place any archaeological find in the context of mankind's development, one must have three basic kinds of facts: placement in space, placement in complexity, and placement in time. Archaeological facts become meaningful only in the light of at least one (preferably all) of these generalizing categories.

Placement in Space

The archaeologist is concerned with determining the area occupied by a prehistoric people (tribe, nation, racial group) because this information may be important in determining the effects of trade, contact with other peoples, the economic base for the group, and sometimes such things as political organization. Present political boundaries between nations may confuse this placement, since they do not coincide with ancient boundaries. The Maya Indians and their forebears, who established one of the New World civilizations, occupied parts of Mexico, Guatemala, British Honduras, Honduras, and Salvador. Their territory bore no relation to the present mapped boundary lines.

Finding the geographical extent of prehistoric cultures is simple in theory, but like many other phases of archaeology, may be different in practice. If previous archaeological work has been done in the region, an archaeologist can check his finds against books and records to find out where the same kinds of implements have been found. If no archaeological information is available, the task at hand is to gather primary data; area comparisons must await the accumulation of information. Determination of ancient boundary lines around culture units is often a near-impossible task because for most of the world the archaeological resources have yet to be found and published.

Even when relatively much archaeological information is available, many problems arise in figuring cultural boundaries. No large group of people is uniform, and the archaeologist must decide how large the differences must be before they can be deemed differences of a tribal or national character. In the case of the Maya, for example, people living in outlying regions did not put up the inscribed stone monuments characteristic of the central groups, nor did they erect stone buildings. The ruins in some areas are therefore quite different from the central pattern, yet the people were the same. In this case the boundary is determined by similarities in pottery and small objects, plus historical accounts and knowledge of the area within which the Mayan language was used.

As we plot the distribution of artifacts (such as particular types of arrowheads) or cultural features (such as art styles) on a map and notice that similar traits have been found in widely separated spots, we are face to face with a central problem for archaeologists — that of evaluating similarities in terms of cultural connections. If we find pyramids in Egypt and pyramids in Mexico, does this fact indicate that people from one of these places must have carried the idea to the other place? If we find large stone heads in South America, on Easter Island, and also in Polynesia, are they evidences of historic connection? Very different answers are made to this kind of question. It is therefore easy to see why one of the archaeologist's chief tasks is to understand the spatial relationships of ancient people and to interpret the similarities and differences of their cultures.

Similarities cannot be interpreted according to any clearly defined rule, hence there is controversy among modern scholars. Some hold that independent discovery explains most of the similarities that can be seen. Others propose that almost any likeness is evi-

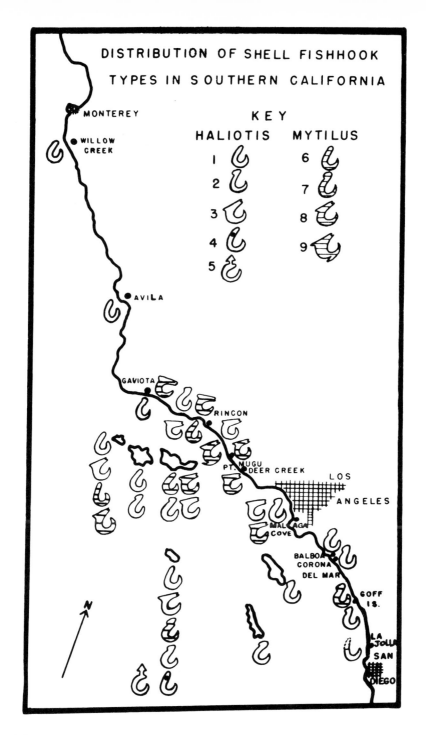

Fig. 3. A distribution map. *This map shows the locations in southern California yielding shell fishhooks from archaeological sites. Reproduced from M. Wissler, "A Canalino Site near Deer Canyon, Ventura County, California," The Masterkey, Vol. 32, No. 3 (1958). By permission of the Southwest Museum.*

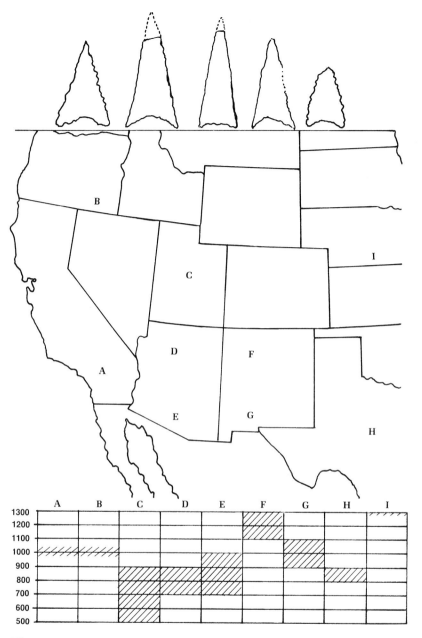

Fig. 4. Distribution map. *This type of map shows the distribution in both time and space of a class of artifacts, in this case a kind of arrow point. The location of reported finds is shown on a map of the western United States by the letters. At bottom, the evident ages are indicated on the chart (dates A.D.). Such placement in time and space permits historical conclusions about the origin and spread of a particular idea or feature. This map suggests that the point type in question originated in the central Great Basin about 1,500 years ago and spread to other regions over a period of several hundred years. Reproduced by permission of H. Eberhart from his Ph.D. dissertation at University of California, Los Angeles: "Time Markers in Southern California Archaeology" (1957).*

dence of contact between peoples. Most archaeologists adopt an intermediate position — if the objects compared are technically simple and are inherently limited in their variations, then similarities between two regions could result *either* from borrowing or from independent discovery. An arrow point, for example, needs a pointed end and is therefore nearly always triangular in basic shape. No connection between two areas need be assumed because triangular arrow points are found in both. Even so, the use of such points may have been transmitted from one group to the other. In such cases, it is not possible to demonstrate which answer is correct.

On the other hand, if the objects compared are complex, with many points of resemblance (such as details of the clothing and ornament of a clay figurine), the chances of independent invention are much smaller and communication between peoples is indicated. For example, finding parts of an American-made Singer sewing machine in central Africa is substantially conclusive evidence of connection with the United States no matter how diffuse or roundabout the connection might be. For other examples not so clearly understood, the arguments may be long and loud.

In studying relationships, it is necessary to base conclusions on more than a single artifact or trait. Similarities between assemblages are more significant than isolated trait similarities. For example, two dry caves a hundred miles apart may yield arrowheads of the same kind, sandals and basketry woven by the same technique, and similar simple wooden objects like the drills used for making fire. Such a similarity in pattern may be convincing evidence of relationship, even though the individual objects are simple in manufacture and so widely used that they would be of little significance taken individually.

Yet the spatial distribution of even single features can be informative, as indicated in the distribution map (Fig. 3). We would expect the occurrence of this particular artifact type (shell fishhooks) to be associated with water and fishing, but the occurrence of the hooks only along certain areas of coast line suggests a cultural distinction between this region and adjacent areas where other styles of fishing implements were used. More comparisons with other elements are necessary before one can decide whether the distinction is correlated with tribal or political boundaries. A different sort of distribution map, shown in Fig. 4, presents both time and space distribution.

Placement in Complexity

An important question about an ancient culture is its place in the progression of human development. The answer involves recognition of historical developments within the culture as well as outside relationships. The understanding of a single culture in relation to the history of mankind as a whole depends necessarily upon a broad knowledge of human developments in many areas and periods. However, two principal aspects of cultural complexity or level of development may be mentioned here.

First, *origins:* We are curious to know when and where the basic features of modern life got their start. Who developed the first writing and when? What group was the first to turn to farming as a means of survival? Where is the first evidence for political "empires"? The answers to such questions tell us the history of man's cultural development. They also provide keys to the understanding of particular cultures, their growth and change. Some cultures tend to originate change through internal inventiveness and adaptation to changing conditions (such as increasingly arid environment). Other cultures seem to be changed more readily from without as foreign ideas are introduced or forced upon them (as with the spread of Roman civilization to tribal groups). Recognition of origins or "first occurrences" permits an evaluation of inventiveness and indicates the regions and periods in which dynamic culture change occurred.

Second, *dimensions of change:* Why do some peoples develop elaborate technologies and others do without them? Why do some cultures change rapidly and others slowly? What are the essential conditions for change to take place? How much choice does a human group have in directing its change? These are questions of great interest, and the archaeologist, through his comparative methods and long-range view of increasing complexity through time, should be able to contribute significant insight to such problems.

Placement in Time

The archaeologist asks and is asked, "How old is it?" For locating archaeological finds in time, a whole series of specialized techniques and methods have been developed. Table 2 summarizes the principal dating methods.

From the dating methods now available, including many techniques not listed in the table that have local but not general

TABLE 2. PRINCIPAL DATING METHODS APPLIED TO ARCHAEOLOGY

Basis	Maximum time span	Remarks
1. Inscriptions	About 5,000 years. Not useable in most of the world due to absence of writing.	Generally very reliable if available.
2. Time markers (see text for explanation)	Theoretically no limit; in practice not often useable before 12,000 to 18,000 years ago because artifacts are too simple.	Used with discrimination can be good approximation of time.
3. Rate of deposition (natural or hidden accumulations)	No limit.	Can yield right answer but generally unreliable.
4. Chemical changes in soil, shell, or bone; also weathering of artifacts	No limit.	Useful for relative dating but gives only very general information.
5. Association with geological feature of known date (volcanic eruption, floods, etc.)	No limit.	Very useful in some areas.
6. Dendrochronology	About 2,000 years in S.W. United States, somewhat less in a few other regions. Not used in many areas.	Excellent reliability, precise date often obtainable.
7. Radiocarbon (carbon-14)	About 40,000 years; good prospects that this range will be increased.	Has yielded wrong answers but generally correct and quite useful.

application, the archaeologist can usually make a fairly close determination of age. Usually the archaeologist is concerned with many measurements of age and devotes much of his time to answering chronological questions, all of which are important in making conclusions about historical processes. The "how old?" question may have many aspects.

1. *Time spans.* Dates for the beginning and end of a site occupation are needed, and also dates for events and cultural changes

that took place during a long time span. Beginning and end may be enough for villages or structures that survived only a year or so: for example, a Spanish mission in California destroyed by Indian uprising two years after it was built. More dates are wanted for objects from sites where people have been living almost continuously for thousands of years, as in many Near Eastern localities.

2. *Internal and external dating.* The evidence for dates may be internal or external. The layering of site material as soil and refuse accumulate, the superposition of one building on the ruins of another, and similar stratigraphy are examples of internal evidence. The finding in one site of coins, pottery, or other objects from other sites are examples of external evidence. Either kind of evidence may serve to establish relative or specific dates.

3. *Field dating and laboratory dating.* Some of the age determinations depend upon observations made by the field worker in the course of excavation; others depend upon chemical or physical tests that can be done only in a laboratory. The excavator must get what chronological information he can while the digging is going on, but he must also collect and preserve those things useful for laboratory testing, such as charcoal, soil samples, and the like.

4. *Long-range and short-range dating.* For the age of very ancient objects, approximate dates are usually sufficiently precise. The geological methods (3, 4, and 5 in Table 2) are usually satisfactory for dating these; a difference of a century or a millenium seldom matters for a paleolithic camp site. Methods that provide greater precision must be used for more recent objects; a difference of a century might be a serious matter in dating a medieval building.

A brief description of some useful techniques for determining age follows. Bear in mind that the archaeologist can sometimes use several of these at the same site, and that his notebooks will assemble many kinds of chronological information as part of the data-gathering process.

One apparently easy way of determining the age of a find is by an inscription left by the maker of the object. Objects such as monuments or coins may bear dates. However, determining age by such dating is less easy than some may imagine. A monument neatly inscribed "A.U.C. DCLII" will rarely be found. A written inscription must be deciphered to be of any use, and is of limited use unless it can be converted into the present-day calendar. It is fairly easy to learn that A.U.C. DCLII is about 101 B.C.— but what about "the sixth year of the reign of the king Isin"?

Another dating method is secondary dating based upon the discovery of objects of known date. Through the years archaeologists have been able to define a great many *time markers* — distinctive objects known to have been manufactured during a limited time span, and hence significant wherever found. Many pottery types, ornaments, and other artifacts are useful as time markers because they change rapidly (usually for reasons of style or popularity). As trade objects they are particularly useful in dating. One example is a kind of faience (blue-glazed) bead of Egyptian manufacture known to date from about 1400 B.C. These distinctive beads have also been found far from Egypt, in archaeological sites of Poland, Austria, Spain, France, and Britain. They date any context in which they occur as later than but probably somewhere near 1400 B.C.

Several ways of figuring age have been borrowed from other sciences: knowledge of chemical changes, geological changes, and the rate of soil accumulation may sometimes yield a guess on the age of a find. There are several uncontrolled factors in each of these dating techniques, however, and reliable answers cannot often be attained.

The greatest advance in dating was the development of the radiocarbon method, referred to as the carbon-14 or radioactive-carbon method. This discovery, a by-product of nuclear research, was made by W. F. Libby of the University of Chicago in the 1940's and has since been improved and put into operation in a score of laboratories. Professor Libby, now at the University of California (Los Angeles) was awarded the Nobel Prize for the development of this most ingenious dating method. It depends on changes in the ratio of radioactive carbon-14 to ordinary carbon-12 in organic objects. This ratio is a constant in living matter and decreases at a known rate after a living object dies. Hence measurement of the ratio in an organic specimen permits the age of the specimen to be calculated. The method can be applied to the dating of such things as wood, charcoal, plant fiber, bone, and shell up to 40,000 years old, with some promise that more refined laboratory techniques may permit dating of samples up to 60,000 or 70,000 years in age.

Since charcoal from cooking fires is commonly found in prehistoric camps, even when other organic material is absent, radiocarbon dating has indicated the age of a wide range of archaeological finds all over the world, including many that previously could not be dated.

Radiocarbon dates are published in several places; some examples here given come from the *Radiocarbon Supplement* of the *American Journal of Science* (Vols. 1 and 2). These reports of dates appear in the following form :

M-811 (University of Michigan): Lehner Mammoth Site, Arizona
11,290 ±500*

Mixed pine, ash and oak charcoal from the Lehner Mammoth Site (31°25′23″ N Lat, 110°6′48″ W Long), Cochise County, Arizona. The sample was taken from the second of two hearths on a sand bar in association with an extensive deposit of bones and considerable cultural material. The hearth was buried under fine sand, swamp soil, silts grading to clayey silt — post-Altithermal and recent deposits — to a depth of about 3 m. The fauna represented in the bone deposits included nine young mammoths and bone elements of horse, bison and tapir. The associated cultural material included thirteen Clovis fluted points and eight cutting and scraping tools presumed to have been used in butchering. Collected 1956 by W. W. Wasley, submitted by E. W. Haury, University of Arizona, Tucson, who has published a description of the site.

BM-56 (British Museum): Mycerinus, Gizeh   1500 ±150

Human skin from the body of a man (now in the British Museum) found by H. Raven when working for Col. Howard Vyse in 1838 in the Pyramid of Mycerinus, Gizeh (29°58′ N Lat, 31°07′30″ E Long) Egypt. Submitted by I. E. S. Edwards, Keeper of the Department of Egyptian Antiquities, British Museum. . . . The result disposes of the suggestion that the body is that of King Mycerinus which had been placed in a new coffin about 600 B.C.

Several thousand radiocarbon dates are now published. Two published sources now summarize radiocarbon dates annually. One is a file of edge-punched cards published by Radiocarbon Dates Association, Inc., Andover, Massachusetts; the other is the journal *Radiocarbon* (formerly *Radiocarbon Supplement*) published by Yale University.

---

* The number M-811 is that of the sample as given by the laboratory at the University of Michigan. The figure 11,290±500 is the number of years before the age determination.

The radiocarbon method has some drawbacks, chiefly the fact that it can be applied only to organic substances. In many of the older sites, only stone tools and similar nonorganic items are found, and there is no way of dating these by radiocarbon. There is also a chance of contamination in some samples so that it is possible to get a wrong answer. The method requires the assumption that the carbon ratio in ancient living matter is the same as that in presently living matter — a safe but not certain probability. It remains among the most useful of modern archaeological techniques, however, and the whole study of prehistory has been tremendously advanced by this discovery.

Another precise method of dating has the scientific name of dendrochronology (from Greek *dendron,* tree, and *chronos,* time), popularly called tree-ring dating. The system was developed by the astronomer A. E. Douglass in 1913 for an entirely different purpose. Douglass was interested in the correlation of tree-growth patterns with cycles of sun-spot occurrences. In favorable years, the growing tree makes wider rings than in unfavorable years; a series of growth rings thus corresponds to a series of local climate variations. The series of varying rings can be matched and overlapped as shown in Fig. 6 to establish dates quite far back in time. Much effort is required to set up the original calendar, for one must begin with trees now living and work backwards with older and older wood samples, overlapping the ring patterns until the maximum time depth is reached. Once established, the master chart for a given area can be used to date wood samples whose rings match a portion of the over-all calendar. Where such a master chart has been completed, it is sometimes possible to date the construction of a building, for example, to within a year or two.

Tree-ring dates are compiled in the *Tree Ring Bulletin,* published at the University of Arizona (Tucson). Examples (from Vol. 17, No. 4, p. 27) are given as follows:

Site	Cultural stage	Dated specimens	Dated rooms	Range of dates
Awatovi	Pueblo III-IV	468	53	A.D. 1223± 20 to 1700
Site 264	Basket Maker III-Pueblo I	86	10	A.D. 659 to 816

Like other dating methods, tree-ring dating has certain problems that prevent its universal use. Relatively few areas of the world

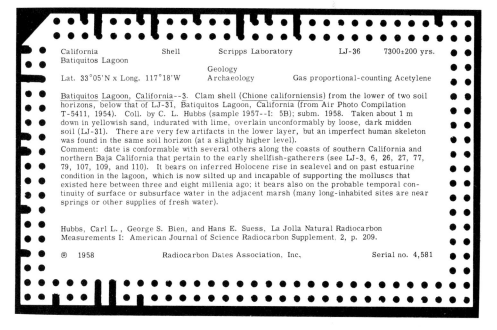

Fig. 5. A radiocarbon record on a keysort card. *Note the extreme care with which location of the site is recorded, and other details of systematic scientific technique. The card is 5 inches by 8 inches. The punched-out slots and holes enable the card user to find cards by mechanical methods without examining all cards in the file. Reproduced by permission of Dr. Frederick Johnson and Radiocarbon Dates Association, Inc.*

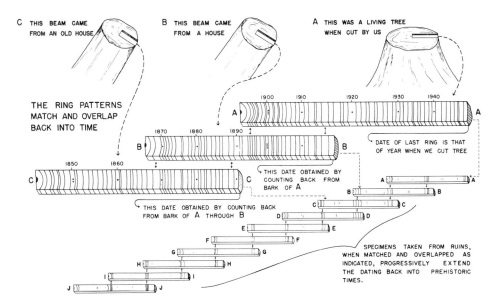

Fig. 6. Dendrochronology. *Diagram showing how the pattern of tree rings is used to build a chronology and determine the age of ancient wood specimens. Reproduced from W. S. Stallings, Jr.,* Dating Prehistoric Ruins by Tree-Rings, *Laboratory of Tree Ring Research, University of Arizona, 1949. By permission of the laboratory and Dr. Bryant Bannister.*

yield large pieces of wood in archaeological contexts. Some trees, because of their even growth in good and bad years, do not develop the sequence patterns needed for comparison; such wood growth is referred to as "complacent" and cannot be used to derive a date.

In practice, dendrochronology has been most useful in the southwestern part of the United States, where the dry climate preserves many ancient timbers and where marked fluctuations in rainfall have left a clear record in the growth pattern of the wood. Here villages dating back almost 2,000 years have been precisely dated. In recent years, there has been progress in other parts of the world in establishing tree-ring calendars for their local conditions, and the tree-ring method may be a most valuable one in any district where many pieces of wood are preserved and where climatic fluctuations are clearly recorded in the tree growths.

New ways of determining age are constantly being sought by archaeologists. No known methods can be applied to all finds in all areas, and often several techniques are needed to determine age. Experimental dating methods under study include a technique for determining the age of pottery objects and another for determining the age of obsidian objects.

In addition, the success of the radiocarbon methods of age determination has stimulated a search for other dating methods based upon the decay rate of radioactive isotopes other than carbon-14. Any chemical or physical change that proceeds at a constant and measurable rate is potentially an indicator of age. Eventually, archaeologists hope to have a battery of techniques that should permit them to determine the age of almost any find.

Finally, in addition to the techniques mentioned above, all of which are *absolute* in that they yield an age in terms of "years ago," a date in our calendar system, there are methods of *relative* dating, in which finds may be placed in a sequence without knowing how old the sequence is. The most common such method is the studying of superposition — the layers deposited first must be the oldest, and the levels above must come later in time. This explains why archaeologists are so careful to record the depth at which objects are found — the depth usually has a bearing on the age of the find, at least in relating it to other finds from the same site.

Interpreting the Records

Archaeologists are more interested in information about the peoples who once occupied the site of a digging than in collecting treasures.

Like a detective, the archaeologist searches for clues in order to discover and reconstruct something that happened. Like the detective, the archaeologist finds no clues too small or insignificant. And like the detective, the archaeologist must usually work with fragmentary and often confusing information. Finally, the detective and the archaeologist have as their goal the completion of a report, based on a study of their clues, that not only tells what happened but proves it.

What, then, are the clues that make up the records of the past, and how can they be read? They are seldom literal documents, although ancient written records are found in some parts of the world. But whether or not written records are found, the archaeologist always has available two kinds of documents. The first and most important are the *material remains* left behind by the people. These include not only buildings and monuments, but also skeletons of the people in their graves, offerings placed with them, and objects lost, thrown away, broken, discarded, or for some other reason buried in the earth and uncovered, years later, by the archaeologist. The material remnants are not only objects made by the people, such as tools and ornaments, but also their refuse — animal bones, shells, and similar material — which give valuable information about food sources.

A second and equally important kind of document in addition to the material objects themselves is the relationship between objects found in the same place. This *context of discovery* often provides the only evidence for the use and meaning of the artifact. For example, there is a class of small ornaments called labrets, usually made of stone, worn in a hole perforated in the lower lip. They are often spool-shaped, although other forms also occur. But a small stone object of spool shape is not necessarily a labret: it could be an ear ornament, part of a necklace, or perhaps even part of a functional tool. The only way one can be confident that objects of this kind are labrets is to find one in position against the buried skull, resting where the lower lip used to be, and suggesting that the dead individual was buried wearing an ornament of this kind. The physical object is a document in itself, but it may be a meaningless document, or a misleading document, without the evidence provided by the context — the relationship of the labret to the skull.

In passing, it may be mentioned that destruction of context is precisely the source of the resentment archaeologists feel toward amateur relic collectors and those who plunder sites in order to obtain art objects. It is a very sad thing to realize that most of the treasures of prehistoric art in collections, including those in art museums, were excavated unscientifically, removed from their context, and sold as contraband to a collector. For objects of artistic merit may also be particularly important scientifically. Since the skill and care of their manufacture indicates them to be highly valued by their makers, the context of such finds could be especially informative about the people who made them. Unfortunately, many of the most beautiful archaeological finds are stripped of informative value except for a one-line label indicating the part of the world from which they came.

For the archaeologist to "read" the documents of material objects, he must at each find ask questions about its use, its manufacture, and its origin.

In Fig. 7 are two stone points. We can begin to read this archaeological document by exploring the questions given above. The use of the longer one seems obvious; surely the point was used as the tip of an arrow or perhaps a spear. Yet such an interpretation is incorrect, for this particular find is in fact a stone knife. The interpretation is confirmed by a relationship situation. The object was found in a house that had been destroyed by fire. In the opposite corner of the house was discovered a second stone point, similar in size and shape to the one illustrated. The second one (the wider), however, was found with a short wooden handle preserved in carbonized form. Since the first example was found in the same house and is of the same size and shape, it may be inferred that it also is a knife rather than a projectile weapon. The inference is almost certain because the base of the example in question shows a discolored area where a wide wooden handle had burned away.

The question of *manufacture* is in part answered when it is observed that the point was made by chipping off small flakes

Fig. 7. Archaeological documents interpreted from their context. *Stone knives from the Paragonah pit house (Figs. 78–85). The one on the left is discolored at the base where a wide wooden handle burned away. The one on the right (to smaller scale) had the wooden handle preserved in carbonized form. The blades are of chalcedony and parts are missing because of breakage in the fire that destroyed the house.*

Fig. 8. Copper bells found with a prehistoric burial in Nayarit, Mexico. *The use and meaning of such archaeological finds is less clear than those of tools which had a function interpretable from their form.*

from the surface. The method by which this is done is called pressure flaking; a small pointed object, usually bone or antler, is pressed against the edges and surface to force off small chips. Stone points indicate a relatively simple technology, but this chipping technique is by no means the most crude and simple for the shaping of stone objects. Hence looking into the question of manufacture leads to some understanding of the level of technological skill possessed by the people of this particular time and place.

The third question, the *origin* of the artifact, is important in showing sources of outside contact and trade. An obvious way to answer the question in this case is to examine the material of which the point is made and then discover where such material can be obtained. In this case, the stone knife is made of a glassy pink and white chalcedony known to occur as an outcrop on a high mountain only a few miles from where the knife was found. This particular specimen, therefore, gives no indication that the people roamed very far from home or traded material from a distance.

The same kind of reasoning can be applied to a slightly more difficult case, the objects illustrated in Fig. 8, some copper bells. Again the use appears deceptively obvious, but the number of possible uses is greater than in the case of the knife. Was this bell an ornament worn by an important person? Was it a part of a string of bells worn around the ankle of a dancer to provide noisy accompaniment to the dance steps? Was it used in a temple to accompany religious ceremonies? Or was it a standard of exchange, a kind of money that could be used to trade for desired objects? It could have been used in any of these or in dozens of other possible ways. Again the only way in which an accurate conclusion can be reached is through observation of the context of the discovery. In this case, the bell was found with several others arranged around the leg bones of a skeleton. Its use, therefore, was probably ornamental.

The bell was made by the lost-wax process, in which a model is first made in wax, the model encased in clay, and molten metal poured in to melt the wax model and replace it. Considerable technological skill is indicated, not only in the casting process but also in obtaining the metal to be cast.

The question of where the bell came from cannot be answered at present. A detailed metallurgical analysis might reveal trace elements that would identify the source of the copper. Or, it

Fig. 9. Pottery figurines from a prehistoric grave in Colima, Mexico. *Such figures are informative about details of clothing and ornament, but their meaning to the people who made them is most difficult for the archaeologist to unravel since a multitude of meanings is possible for objects which are not tools or used in a functional sense. (Note the scale, here in centimeters. It is sound technique always to include a scale-showing object in photographs like this.)*

might be possible through comparison of the style of the bell with bells of other areas to locate the place of origin. However, at present no answer is possible for this particular example, and several unresolved questions remain that can be answered only from examination of similar objects and from comparative research.

As a final example, consider an object that has no apparent "use" in the tool sense, the pottery figurines in Fig. 9. Here the question of use is secondary to the question of meaning, since the figurines must have had significance to the makers, and a correct reconstruction of past history involves recognition of what this significance may have been. Although the clay images could not have been used physically like a tool, they could well have been viewed as utilitarian in a magical or religious sense — that is, they could have been made to accomplish something (as in sorcery, for example). But since there is seldom anything in a physical object of this kind to indicate its meaning, one must again rely almost entirely on archaeological context for clues to interpretation.

To appreciate the difficulties of interpreting such objects, consider *some* of the things they may have been:

1. Idols for household use, to which propitiatory offerings were made
2. Votive offerings to insure the success of some venture
3. Dedicatory offerings at a construction ceremony of temple or monument
4. Thank offerings for divine favors granted
5. Mortuary furniture — offerings to the dead
6. Dolls or playthings
7. Amulets, fetishes, or "good-luck pieces" to be worn or carried
8. Fertility emblems
9. Objects used in witchcraft or black magic (symbols of an enemy to be destroyed)
10. Objects used in sympathetic or imitative magic for general or specific fertility
11. Ceremonial gifts
12. Trade items
13. Servant images to care for the dead in the underworld

All of these functions, and more, have been applied to human figurines by different peoples. But what of the archaeological context? The figures in the illustration were found in a grave although many fragments of identical figures were found in domestic debris (including potsherds, animal bones, and general dwelling refuse). About the only conclusion that can be drawn is that the image must have had some meaning appropriate for burial with an adult, even though many such figures apparently could not have had more than transitory importance since they were readily discarded. Both the style of manufacture and the type of clay indicate that the figure was made locally (in western Mexico), so these are not helpful in formulating interpretation. Frustrating though it may be, if this find is the only source of information it would have to be admitted that the archaeologist can only surmise the meaning — he does not and cannot know the figurine's significance.

A discouragingly large number of archaeological finds are in this enigmatic category and can be interpreted only in terms of possible or probable meaning. The archaeologist must speculate and use his knowledge to yield the best inference. But this inference is not mere blind guessing — the archaeologist usually has other finds of similar material for comparison, and he is able to suggest analogies to the customs of living primitive peoples. Even though he cannot always prove his interpretation, he can often suggest a plausible explanation for his finds.

The foregoing examples show how the archaeologist can read the information available to him and also show some of the limitations of archaeological interpretation. It is apparent that it is easier to figure the use of things that are tools, such as knives, than it is to interpret less functional objects such as copper bells. The less functional the object appears to be, the more interpretations are possible. One must beware of accepting the first simple explanation and must explore many alternatives in studying artifacts recovered from prehistoric sites.

It is also evident from the examples that the archaeologist must draw on diverse kinds of knowledge in order to understand his finds. In the case of the stone point, it is necessary to know something about the local geology to interpret the source. For the copper bell one must know something about metallurgical processes and techniques, and for the human figurine something about ceramics and artistic style. The best archaeologists have a wide knowledge, not only of the customs of living primitive peoples, but also of local history, geology, biology, and specialized subjects in both the cultural and natural sciences.

The most important single source of knowledge required for interpretation of archaeological finds is ethnography — the description of the cultures of living peoples including those with primitive technologies and customs very different from those of modern civilizations. Most archaeological interpretation is based directly on the assumption that the use and meaning of archaeological specimens was similar to their use and meaning among primitive peoples found to be using such objects now or in the recent past. One may question such an assumption, but it appears to be generally valid, and in any case there is no other way to draw reasonable interpretations about most archaeological finds.

Even for utilitarian objects, reference to ethnography is important if the archaeologist is to avoid fanciful and often absurd interpretations. Some examples show this point very well — one is reported by the British archaeologist Clark, who studied a number of enigmatic wooden objects found preserved in the peat bogs of northern Europe (Fig. 10). These had been interpreted in various ways (one archaeologist thought they were musical instruments) until Clark discovered that similar devices were being used by peasants as deer traps. Interpreting these objects as musical instruments might have led to a correspondingly erroneous reconstruction of the past. Reference to historical and ethnographic data here put the archaeologist on the right approach.

A second example is even more direct. At several locations in the foothills of the Sierra Nevada of California, archaeologists had found pitted stone objects made from fragments of broken soapstone bowls. They speculated at length on what the objects might be. The soft stone (it can be scratched with the fingernail) seemed to rule out many tool uses. After much guessing and the compilation of a list of "interpretations," none of which seemed convincingly plausible, it occurred to the archaeologists that since the sites in question were relatively recent, a living Indian might know what the artifacts were. And an aged Indian woman immediately recognized the object, looked for and found another one in her front yard, and demonstrated its use by standing acorns in the pits and breaking the shells by tapping them with a pebble. The pitted stones could be rapidly made from the pieces of broken vessels to shell acorns quickly and easily. This example indicates that the best approach to interpretation may be the simplest one — find a user of the device and ask him about it.

But sometimes no user is at hand. The people who were users

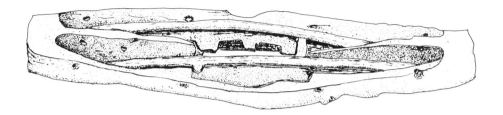

Fig. 10. Tread trap from the peat bogs of the Viborg district, Jutland. *(Redrawn after J. G. D. Clark: Prehistoric Europe, the Economic Basis, Fig. 1c.) Such traps were used to secure deer and similar animals. The trap is a hollowed-out log with two springy branches set into it; concealed in the animal trail, it catches the foot between these springs. Ropes through the holes keep the animal from dragging the trap away. The specimen is about 34 inches long. Numerous archaeological specimens of this kind have been found in northern Europe dating back as far as 2,500 years ago. Archaeologists had great difficulty identifying these objects and misinterpreted them in various ways — Clark mentions musical instruments, machines for making peat bricks, models of boats, and devices for catching fish.*

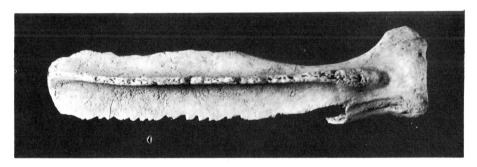

Fig. 11. Notched-bone "saw" (length 6 inches) from an archaeological site in central California. *These objects are made from the shoulder blade of a deer and are relatively common in archaeological sites of the West Coast dating within the last thousand years and down to the recent past. Though many Europeans and Americans must have seen these tools in use, no written record of them is known. Archaeologists have suggested that they may be fish scalers, grass cutters, or devices for preparing animal skins. Without a precise ethnographic analogy, the archaeologist often cannot identify the objects he digs up.*

may have died out or may have given up the old ways in favor of modern conveniences; or the existing users may live in another part of the world. In such cases, the archaeologist employs the "ask the user" approach indirectly. That is, he consults ethnographic records, reports of the customs and activities of primitive or other peoples investigated by ethnologists and anthropologists.

Where no ethnographic record exists, interpretation of simple objects is often very difficult. Another Californian example (also found widely in the western United States) is a device called a scapula "saw" (Fig. 11). Made from the shoulder blades (scapulas) of deer, these objects are standard in form and usually show polish and sometimes extensive wear on the notched edge. It is clear that they were utilitarian, but for what use? Archaeologists have inferred such uses as fish scaling and grass cutting, but so far these interpretations are tentative and uncertain because no eyewitness record of the use of such tools seems to be preserved.

When the archaeologist faces interpretation of objects having nontangible use (items of magical or social meaning, for example), the ethnographic record becomes even more important. How can the archaeologist, product of a civilized, urban society, interpret something that does not exist in his own life (witchcraft, for example)? Here again knowledge of simpler peoples provides a basis for interpretation. Without such knowledge interpretations may well be naive, farfetched, or completely fantastic — at best, mere guesses originating in the mind of the archaeologist. When ethnographic knowledge can be used, a more convincing explanation can be made, as in the case of certain figurines from a cave in Arizona described by the archaeologist E. H. Morris. Morris reported clay figurines stuck full of cactus spines. From reference to many places in the world where primitive peoples believe that injurious treatment of an image will harm a real person, Morris interpreted the figurines as instances of witchcraft or black magic. Such an interpretation is quite convincing; although it can never be proved (and could be wrong), the interpretation seems the most probable one in view of a common belief pattern among tribal peoples.

In writing their reports, archaeologists are likely to cite the interpretations of other archaeologists and to work from context of the archaeological finds rather than make direct reference to historical and ethnographic information. The reader of archaeological reports (and sometimes the writer) may, therefore, not fully appreciate the dependence of the archaeologist on such data. However, nearly all archaeological interpretations are ultimately based on comparison with observed or reported customs.

Practical evidence of this dependence on ethnography is the number of archaeologists who take academic work in anthropology and the fact that the best archaeologists spend much of their time studying ethnographic and historical records. These range from the travel accounts of Herodotus, the Greek who visited Egypt and the Near East about 450 B.C., to descriptions of the present life of American Indians, pygmies in Africa, and Australian aborigines.

Unfortunately for the archaeologist, modern anthropology is more concerned with social theory than with careful recording of artifacts and practices; the ethnographies most useful to the achaeologist are those of previous generations, whose attention to descriptive detail grew from a natural-science approach as distinguished from social-science emphasis. The archaeologist cannot make the social interpretation of his data until he can recognize and interpret the objects he finds, and it is regrettable that in the modern world many aboriginal technologies are disappearing with no record of them being made.

SOME GENERAL WORKS DEALING WITH ARCHAEOLOGICAL METHODS AND TECHNIQUES

ATKINSON, R. J. C.

1953   *Field Archaeology*. Methuen, London. Basic field methods; includes discussion of electrical devices for locating buried features, and practical information on preparing for publication.

CHILDE, V. G.

1956a   *Piecing together the Past*. Praeger, New York.

1956b   *A Short Introduction to Archaeology*. Frederick Muller, London. Two essays by a noted British archaeologist, primarily concerned not with field methodology but with Childe's view of the context and intellectual approach to archaeological studies.

CLARK, GRAHAME (also published as CLARKE, GRAHAM)

1947   *Archaeology and Society*. Methuen, London. One of the better introductory books for relating interpretation to methodology.

GRIFFIN, JAMES B., ed.

1951   *Essays in Archaeological Methods*. Museum of Anthropology,

University of Michigan, Occasional Papers No. 8. Ann Arbor. A series of articles by several archaeologists discussing selected topics dealing with field and laboratory methods.

HEIZER, R. F., ed.

1959a   *A Manual of Archaeological Field Methods.* National Press, Palo Alto, California. Field excavation techniques explained by a group of California students. The book has been used for several years and with various revisions made in the newer editions. It is one of the most useful "how to dig" books.

1959b   *The Archaeologist at Work.* Harper, New York. A series of reprinted articles in which archaeologists tell how they solved various problems of excavation and analysis.

KENYON, KATHLEEN M.

1952   *Beginning in Archaeology.* Phoenix House, London. A British field manual detailing excavation methods.

MEIGHAN, C. W.

1961   *The Archaeologist's Note Book.* Chandler, San Francisco. Following a brief introduction to excavation methods, the bulk of the notebook consists of printed forms designed to facilitate recording of the main kinds of archaeological remains discovered by the field worker. Primarily a record book to be filled in by the excavator.

PETRIE, W. M. F.

1904   *Methods and Aims in Archaeology.* Macmillan, London. One of the first books dealing with this subject, this volume is still worth reading for its excellent statement of the archaeologist's view of his study. Petrie was one of the pioneers in the scientific archaeology of Egypt.

PIGGOTT, STUART

1959   *Approach to Archaeology.* Harvard University Press, Cambridge, Mass. Describes basic field and interpretative techniques with emphasis on European examples.

WHEELER, M.

1954   *Archaeology from the Earth.* Clarendon Press, Oxford. An excellent summary concentrating on field methodology and the organization and strategy of archaeological exploration.

PROFESSIONAL SOCIETIES AND PUBLICATIONS

American Journal of Archaeology
Archaeological Institute of America, 5 Washington Square North, New York, N.Y. 10003.

American Antiquity
Society for American Archaeology, 1530 P St., N.W., Washington, D.C. 20005.

3 LOWER PALEOLITHIC MAN:
Tools and Cultures

When in the course of time a space ship returns from the moon or from another planet with observers, everyone will be excited and impressed by this (for a time) highest achievement of our technological history — surpassing the first engine, the first airplane, and other landmarks. But it may not, in significance, surpass the stone picked up by our cave-man ancestors and used as the first war weapon, hunting missile, or nut cracker.

Yet the first and most important step toward the devices of modern man was made by that very remote ancestor who first utilized a rude tool, perceived the advantages of what he had done, and proceeded thereafter to select and modify other materials of nature for his own purposes. Tool using and tool making are of the essence of humanity, of being a human rather than a lower animal. Without that first step toward the manipulation of nature for human purposes, the anthropoid would not achieve humanity. One of the beginnings for the separation that marks off human life from the lives of other animals was the first tool; and after the first use of tools, all the rest of man's development is a logical outgrowth: his refined and improved tools, his thinking, his material and intellectual culture.

There is obviously a tremendous gap between the stone tools of ancient man and the complex machines of modern times. But a continuing series of small changes bridges it. From time to time a generation had a genius; nearly all generations had a few people whose ideas built upon and elaborated the knowledge they inherited. Our cultural heritage is the sum of the accomplishments of generations preceding us, not only our immediate ancestors but even more the thousands of unknown ancient men in all corners of the earth who had an idea and somehow transmitted it.

Yet it is a mistake (often made) to portray man as constantly and consciously seeking self-betterment or devoting his energies to making the world a better place for the next generation. On the contrary, many significant ideas have been acquired by accident, by fumbling, or by just fooling around in random play. Important innovations have been ignored or forgotten because no one saw the value of them. Man's development has been and still is to a large extent a groping movement in and out of many blind alleys and with many false starts. It is relatively new for man to seek deliberately for a better life. The long-range planning now evidenced by such undertakings as cancer research and the development of computers has appeared only recently in human history. Nevertheless, for many thousands of years humans have been innovating things and activities to make life easier or somehow better.

The history of man's tools must begin with implements showing alteration, however simple, that can be attributed to human activity. True, there may have been a long period, perhaps tens or hundreds of thousands of years, during which our ancestral humans made regular use of natural objects without changing them — picking up a stone and throwing it at an animal, prying out an edible root with a convenient stick which was then discarded, or breaking into a bees' nest with a handy stone to get at the honey. Such simple kinds of tool-using activity fall short of being human. Apes in captivity can be taught to manipulate such man-made tools as wrenches, keys, and eating utensils. They also learn readily to use sticks for getting at food that is out of reach, and they can stack boxes on top of one another to climb after suspended food. In nature, away from human stimulus, tool use by apes is much more limited. They may occasionally throw things out of trees, use a stick to pry up an edible root, or swat one another with branches (but only in play; if really angry they throw the stick away and use teeth and hands). Though this is tool-using behavior, it is nevertheless insignificant in comparison with the simplest tool use by humans.

Aside from apes and monkeys — the animals most similar to humans — other animals make quite limited and rare use of tools. A few of the better-known examples are worth mention as a contrast to human behavior. In the Galapagos Islands, a small finch (*Cactospiza pallida*) repeatedly uses a twig or cactus thorn to get at grubs hidden in crevices beyond reach of the bird's bill. The bird rejects thorns of too short length, discarding them in favor of longer ones, and a suitable thorn may be carried from tree to tree during the hunting activity. Sea otters sometimes open shellfish by pounding them with a rock. Even some insects may on occasion use tools — the females of one wasp species characteristically pack down the earth of their burrows with a pebble held in the jaws. Interesting as these examples are, they all involve merely the manipulation of objects provided ready-made in nature. None of the animals change natural objects into a more useful form. Thus, although limited examples of tool *using* can be found in the animal kingdom, the deliberate *making* of tools is an attribute peculiar to humans and their immediate precursors. Creative tool making has given puny humans, almost hairless and without fang or claw for protection, their dominance over all other animals species in the world.

THE NEAR-MEN

The first beings to enter the province of the archaeologist were quite different from modern humans in their physical and mental features. No creature now living is quite like any of these ancient manlike and early human forms; we must rely entirely on evidence from fragments of fossil bones and stone tools to reconstruct fragments of their history.

During the earlier part of the Pleistocene period, the so-called Ice Age during which glaciers advanced and retreated, several varieties of near-men lived in South Africa, south of the ice sheets but probably in a more moist climate than the region has today. These creatures have been referred to by such terms as ape-men, man-apes, hominids, and similar terms that attempt to describe their biological position. Because of their limited brain size and presumably limited intelligence, as well as other "primitive" physical features, most authorities have been reluctant to classify the South African finds as true humans. They are classed in the primate order as the family Australopithecinae (southern apes), but while not like modern humans, neither are they like any living apes. Some physical features distinctive to humans were present in the Australopithecinae, including the most important one of erect posture. Apes do not habitually walk on the hind legs; the bones of the Australopithecinae show that they walked erect like modern man. The teeth and pelvic bones are also more human than those of living apes. In sum, the term "near-men" is appropriate for these African animals; they were indeed almost human.

Various claims for the "humanity" of these near-men have been made, including claims that they knew and used fire and tools, and suggestions that they may have had a spoken language. Because of fragmentary and disputed evidence, however, such claims were viewed skeptically until recently. The whole question was reopened with a discovery of major importance, reported in 1959 by L. S. B. Leakey, a British archaeologist who has devoted many seasons of exploration to early remains in the Olduvai Gorge, Tanganyika. Searching through strata in this deep canyon, Mr. Leakey was continuing his studies of a widely found assemblage of very simple stone tools, products of what was called the Oldowan culture. In 1959, Mrs. Leakey made one of the rarest of finds, a fossil human form in direct association with stone tools and bones of hunted animals; she found the remains of a broken skull sticking out of a bank. Investigation established that these were bones of a new-found form of the Australopithecinae and that they lay on a camping area containing crude stone tools of Oldowan type, waste flakes of stone, and bones of rodents, birds, other small forms, and immature animals of larger size.

The hominid remains have been classified by Leakey as belonging to a new genus, to which he gave the name *Zinjanthropus boisei* (the East African area is Zinj in the local language). In some ways it is a primitive representative of the Australopithecinae, having a crest of bone down the center of the skull, a characteristic found in some apes. On the other hand, the teeth show numerous manlike features, and it is assumed that the creature walked erect and shared other features with the African near-men.

Although the tools and the bones of Zinjanthropus were found together, it is not certain whether Zinjanthropus was the maker of the tools or the victim of them, himself being merely a game animal for some more advanced primate. At the time of the discovery, no more advanced creature was known to have lived at the time of Zinjanthropus and therefore this form was considered the only possible maker of the Oldowan tools found with him. In 1964, however, Leakey announced the discovery of a more human fossil form, contemporaneous with Zinjanthropus, which he named *Homo habilis*. This again raises the possibility that Zinjanthropus may have been the victim of the Oldowan tools and that *Homo habilis* was the maker of them. More information is needed to resolve this important question.

The Oldowan tools (Fig. 12) are a kind found in several locations of Africa and Asia. The tools are extremely simple, as we would expect, and consist for the most part of small cobbles of two main varieties: rocks showing battering all over, apparently used for hammering or pounding, and cobbles which have had large flakes knocked off one edge to produce a cutting or chopping edge. The "hammers" may well be the implements used in making the "choppers"; the latter, while rudimentary in their manufacture, are definitely manufactured objects showing that the human trait of tool *making* is present in these early creatures. Since we expect that a period of tool *using* existed before tool *making*, these very ancient finds probably do not represent the oldest actual tools. They do, however, represent the oldest recognizable tools, for anything simpler in manufacture would not be recognizable as a tool.

A dating test on volcanic rock samples from directly above and below the spot where Zinjanthropus was found was made by geologists at the University of California, Berkeley, in 1961. An age of 1,750,000 years was determined. The calculations of age are based on radioactive decay of potassium-40 into calcium-40 and argon-40. Known as the potassium-argon dating method, this technique was used on minerals contained in the volcanic material in which the cultural remains were found —the date does not apply directly to the bones of Zinjanthropus nor to the associated tools. By association, however, the age of the layer should date the fossil and cultural finds. If the date proves to be correct, it shows that Zinjanthropus existed in the Pliocene geological period, even earlier than the beginning of the Pleistocene.

In spite of the uncertainties over the makers of Oldowan tools and the precise age of these tools, they are accepted as the beginnings of human tool making and rank as finds of major impor-

Fig. 12. Oldowan tools from Olduvai Gorge, Africa. *Such tools, made in the time of* Zinjanthropus, *present the oldest evidences of tool making, dating according to recent studies from 1,750,000 years ago. These small pebbles, about 3 inches in diameter, have been used as hammers or, with the removal of coarse flakes from one edge, as chopping and cutting tools. The lower specimen is a bone splinter possibly used as a tool but without human modification, length 2¾ inches. (Compare Figs. 13–15.) Specimens from the Lowie Museum, University of California, Berkeley, through the courtesy of Desmond Clark.*

OBJECTS FROM THE ROYAL CEMETERY AT UR

These precious works attest a high technological skill, much wealth and leisure, and artistic excellence devoted to the support of a ruling class. All specimens are in the University of Pennsylvania Museum. Photographs by P. T. Furst.

Fig. 27

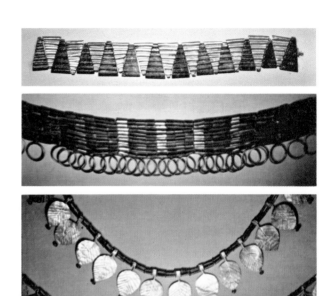

Fig. 31

Fig. 32

Fig. 27. Mosaic plaque from Queen Shubad's tomb. *About 9 inches high. An important personage, seated, is waited on by three attendants.*

Fig. 31. Jewels. *The necklace of beads in the triangle pattern is 2 inches wide. The beads in the necklace with rings are ½ inch long. The greatest length of the gold leaves is 2½ inches.*

Fig. 32. Gold vessels. *The fluted vase is 7 inches tall. The University of Pennsylvania Museum also has a silver vase of the same size and similar design.*

Fig. 33. The sarcophagus. *The inner coffin (Fig. 47) is seen through the slab of plate glass that rests on top of the open sarcophagus.*

Fig. 46   Fig. 53

Fig. 46. Royal shield. *One of the eight shields found in the tomb. It depicts the enemies of Egypt, here shown as Nubians, conquered and subdued. Height 30 inches.*

Fig. 53. Carved and painted ivory plaque. *This object is part of the lid of a storage chest. The scene (height about 12 inches) represents Tutankhamen and his queen.*

Fig. 66

Fig. 68

Fig. 71   Fig. 73

Fig. 66. Fragments of blue-on-white porcelain. *A galleon shipwrecked near the site in 1595 carried Ming porcelain of this type. These pieces are therefore time markers for a probable date of a site level.*

Fig. 68. Five obsidian arrow points. *The principal hunting weapon of the people was the bow and arrow; these points are the tangible evidence. The smallest is just under 1 inch long.*

Fig. 71. Deer-antler tools. *A wedge (left; length between 7 and 8 inches) and an arrow-shaft wrench (right; also see Fig. 70). Wedges are standard woodworking tools, commonly used for splitting logs into planks.*

Fig. 73. "Charmstones." *Polished stones, thought to have been used as hunting charms. These are three of many similar objects found. The one at the left is about 4 inches long.*

Fig. 76. Above: The bones as they were exposed after careful removal of the overburden. *Below:* A Clovis fluted point in position as found. *This point is about 3 inches long and rests against the neck vertebra of a mammoth; it may well have been the cause of the animal's death. The vertebra and other bones, embedded in the site material, are now exhibited in the Arizona State Museum. Photographs by P. T. Furst.*

Fig. 79

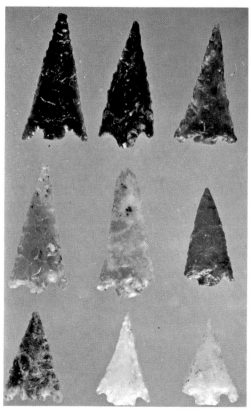

DWELLING
AND ARTIFACTS —
PARAGONAH,
UTAH

Fig. 81

Fig. 79. Model of a pit house. *Compare Fig. 78. The front half is removed to show the reconstructed interior. At the left is the ventilator shaft which provided fresh air for the windowless structure. The roof was built of poles and sticks of graduated size, covered over with a layer of earth. The central cooking fire was under a hole in the roof which also served as a door. These houses often caught fire from rising sparks.*

Fig. 81. Arrow points of obsidian and chalcedony. *The standard hunting weapon for the community, which added much game (mostly deer) to its agricultural economy. The point at upper right is an inch long, others to the same scale. Note that the average size of these points is only a fraction of that for the Clovis points from the Lehner site (Fig. 75). Points used with bow and arrow were in general smaller and lighter than those propelled by a spear thrower.*

Fig. 84

GRAVE
AND
ARTIFACTS—
PARAGONAH,
UTAH

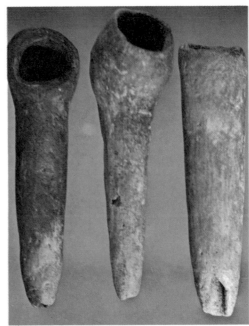

Fig. 86

Fig. 84. A prehistoric burial. *The grave, dug in the floor of a pit house, could be followed exactly because of differences in soil color and texture. No mortuary offerings accompanied this burial, a woman, but other graves at the site contained material offerings of pottery and other objects. Preservation and soil conditions at this site permitted not only the exposure of the exact original contours of the grave excavation but also the completely undisturbed skeleton as shown. Such an exposure of a burial cannot often be made by the archaeologist, because soil conditions, root growth, rodent tunneling, and other causes alter or move the bones after burial.*

Fig. 86. Pottery pipes. *Partly indicative of leisure time enjoyment, but also significant in ritual since tobacco and smoking had sacred connotations for the American Indians, and hence presumably for these Paragonah people as well.*

PAINTED AND
MODELED VESSELS
FROM CEMETERY F,
MOCHE, PERU

Fig. 92

Fig. 91. Figure is presumably a man of rank. *Note the representation of a stirrup-spout pottery vessel. Height of vessel, about 10 inches.*

Fig. 92. Seated figure with numerous ear ornaments. *Height of vessel, about 10 inches.*

Fig. 93. Seated figure with large ear plugs. *Height of vessel, about 7 inches.*

Fig. 91   Fig. 93

Fig. 94   Fig. 95

POTTERY FROM CEMETERY F, MOCHE

Fig. 96   Fig. 97

Fig. 94. Head with feline characteristics, *presumably a deity. Excavated by Uhle. Height of vessel, about 11 inches.*

Fig. 95. Modeled detail. *One of the most lifelike "portraits" in the Uhle collection. The face is about an inch high; the vessel, about 7½ inches.*

Fig. 96. Sleeping figure. *Modeled and painted. A characteristic example of Mochica realism. Height of vessel, just over 6 inches.*

Fig. 97 Painted vessel with stirrup spout. *The scene with two figures may represent divination or some priestly rite. Height of vessel, 9 inches.*

tance for this reason. It seems that these tools and the associated fossil forms must lie very close to the beginnings of human culture — not only are the tools themselves of the maximum simplicity, but the animals hunted appear to have been only small and immature. This evidence suggests that the early hominids were beginning to develop tools but had not obtained the necessary skill to enjoy a real advantage over larger animals such as were hunted by later humans with more advanced tools.

These discoveries also show that beginning culture, the development of tool making, was the product of an animal that was manlike but not "human" in the modern sense of the term. A modern human would see Zinjanthropus as an ape possessed of a few human features; even *Homo habilis* was primitive and apelike in comparison with modern man. The beginnings of culture are therefore much older than creatures physically like modern man. The roots of tool making go far back into our biological ancestry, and the African near-men have a cultural position (as well as a biological position) somewhat intermediate between the modern apes and modern humans. In tool using, at least one form of these near-men had a culture, but one of a crude and limited sort; it stands part way between the rare and random tool using of apes and the deliberate and complex tool making of modern man.

It would appear that the making of tools by the Australopithecinae has been reasonably well demonstrated. The interpretation that they knew the use of fire and had a spoken language are more surprising and less acceptable to many scholars. The evidence for knowledge of fire rests upon chemical analysis of the deposits in which the bones were found, and upon some reportedly charred bones. Evidence of fireplaces has not been found. However, the use of fire goes back some half a million years, as far as Peking man (discussed below) and it may yet develop that this knowledge was present in the era of the Australopithecinae. The question of language may always remain a subject of controversy. Examination of a cast of the inside of the skull, showing the surface of the brain, can reveal the development of the part of the brain connected with speech. However, it is not certain how much development is necessary to permit speech and even if the areas were developed, it is not certain that Australopithecinae talked. Conclusions about the mental development of the Australopithecinae, whose brains were unlike those of any living animal, must remain speculative.

The bare beginnings of humanity revealed in such finds as Zinjanthropus are tantalizing but difficult to assess in terms of modern ideas of culture. The most primitive of humans for whom there is a written observation would be vastly richer in cultural abilities than Zinjanthropus, and at present we can only speculate about the nonmaterial aspects of Zinjanthropus life. To be sure, speculation is based partly upon what is known about recent primitive man and partly upon the life of living nonhuman primates, and it is a fair assumption that the limits of Australopithecine culture fall somewhere between the two. Yet direct evidence from the archaeology is so far very scant and many additional finds are needed before this most interesting incipient culture can be clearly seen.

The adaptation of the Australopithecinae to environment, partly at least through tool use, has been mentioned. Their adaptation to other near-men is unknown. That some sort of family group existed we can be sure, but we cannot say whether it was confined to short periods when the young were infants or whether it was more long-lasting. It is a fair guess that whatever existed in the way of social order was dominated by large males, but there may have been no social order other than animal dominance.

The most interesting and most elusive question is what creatures like Zinjanthropus thought about, or whether they thought about anything. Their tool-making activity is evidence of a brain somewhat more complex than that of living apes, but we do not even know whether Zinjanthropus was human enough to be conscious of his own existence.

If men and their cultures are ranked on the chart of Fig. 2, Zinjanthropus and the other Australopithecinae have their place at the bottom — the beginnings of humanity. Their adaptations can be seen to be very much dominated by "making a living." Social relationships must have occupied a minor part of their time and energy, and so far as we know problems of satisfying the "inner man" had not yet been perceived.

PEKING MAN

Another important discovery of early but definitely human forms was made in China. In a deep limestone cave at Chou Kou Tien, a village near Peking, were found the scattered bones of ancient humans collectively termed Peking man. The physical type of Peking man was found sufficiently different from modern man to classify him as a member of a different zoological group under the scientific name of *Pithecanthropus pekinensis* ("ape man of Peking"). Nonetheless, unlike the Australopithecinae, Peking man was an undoubted human, and all authorities are agreed that he walked erect, made and used a variety of tools, and probably communicated with his neighbors by speaking.

Though the remains of the two beings are widely separated in space and though there is no evidence suggesting direct ancestry or descent, Peking man clearly is later in time than the Australopithecinae. But since geological dates are unsure for either form, we cannot tell yet how long a period elapsed between the two. Still, the age of Peking man is measured in hundreds of thousands of years, and that is enough to place him as a very remote human form. Note that these earliest evidences of human activity are too old to be dated by techniques such as radiocarbon. Development of geological methods such as the potassium-argon method may ultimately solve this dating problem, although this method has not yet been applied to Peking man.

Though some stone tools found in Asia are older than those found with Peking man, Peking man remains one of the most important discoveries for human cultural history, for the same reason as the Zinjanthropus discovery: namely, the association of tools with bones of the tool makers and other clues to life in ancient times. The Peking cave yielded the bones of Peking man, his tools, bones of the animals he ate, and remains of his fireplaces.

All of the known skeletal fragments of Peking man are from this single location, although similar creatures have been found elsewhere in Asia and the crude stone tools are also found more widely. The first discovery of Peking man was reported in 1927 by Davidson Black, a Canadian anatomist working at Peking Union Medical College. Several seasons of excavation between 1927 and 1941 produced thousands of fossil animal bones, stone tools, and the bones of more than thirty humans. Excavation of this extremely important site was hampered by the unsettled political conditions of Asia during the period. The Sino-Japanese war created much difficulty, and with the commencement of World War II the scientific work was halted entirely. Nearly all of the human materials from Chou Kou Tien were lost at the beginning of World War II and have not been located since. The specimens were on a train captured by the Japanese and the present location of the bones and artifacts is unknown. Several detailed reports from the scholars connected with the excavations are available, which describe and illustrate the specimens. Moreover, carefully made casts of the fossils were widely distributed, hence loss of the original specimens does not eliminate scientific study and conclusions. However, loss of the original collections of the artifacts has been a serious hindrance to complete analysis of the cultural activities of Peking man. Although many of the tools are illustrated, further studies could be done if the collections were available. Eventually another collection from Chou Kou Tien or from another site like it will be made, but meanwhile we must rely entirely on the reports of the original scholars.

The occupation of Chou Kou Tien cave covered a long time span, during which the cave gradually filled and the older refuse became buried under later deposits. In the stratigraphy of the cave, the levels from which Peking man's remains were recovered were called Zone C by the discoverers, being beneath two thick layers of limestone deposit. The layer of Zone C contained four classes of objects.

1. Thousands of animal bones, most of which were from food animals hunted by Peking man. Many show breaking and splitting from being cracked to get at the marrow. Most of the animal species are extinct today, although they were fairly abundant in the area during the time of Peking man. The most abundant remains in the cave were from:

   Equus, a horse.
   Rhinoceros (extinct form).
   Cervus pachyosteus, a large deer.
   Elephas namadicus, an extinct elephant species.
   Wild boar (undetermined species).
   Hyaena sinensis, an extinct hyena. This animal was probably not used for food but visited the cave when humans were absent; abundant bones and excrement were found. The hyenas probably dragged other animals into the cave, and they would certainly have consumed any meat left behind by the human occupants.

2. Several thousand stone fragments showing the activities of Peking man. Most are chips and flakes discarded from tool-

making activity, but many finished, although very crude, stone tools were found as well. The stone tools are chipped on only one side. Peking man used pebbles trimmed roughly into shape, and also made occasional use of large coarse flakes struck from the rock. In technological terms, these tools indicate a "chopper industry" not very different from that represented by the ancient African tools previously discussed. Most of the Peking man specimens are quartz, but other materials also occur. There is no real patterning to the manufacture; the tools are crude all-purpose implements, made hastily and discarded readily. There are no tools like spear points or even carefully shaped choppers.

3. Some 75 animal bones showing cutting, scratching, and other working. Some of these are probably tools, although many may be the result of butchering food animals. The worked bones are so crude as to be difficult to interpret. However, there is no reason to think that primitive man, once he began making tools, would confine his efforts to stone, or for that matter that stone tools were first. The experimentation with shaping and using natural materials would of course include wood and bone, although objects of these softer materials are rarely preserved in early sites.

4. The remains of Peking man himself. No complete skeletons were found, but bones of many individuals were present, including persons of both sexes and all ages. People of later times commonly buried their dead in caves, but the bones of Peking man show no intentional burial; it looks as if the dead were simply abandoned without burial preparations. The practice lessens the likelihood of our finding further Peking men, for unburied remains are preserved only under exceptional conditions.

The many objects from Zone C permit several inferences about the achievements of Peking man. Of major importance was the evidence that Peking man had definitely attained the control of fire: the oldest positive evidence. Free bits of charcoal were found in the Zone C debris, but more important was the presence of yellow and red bands of discolored material representing the hearths and fires of Peking man. A few horn cores of *Ovis ammon*, the wild sheep, had been burnt in these fires, although burning is surprisingly scarce on the many bones from the same layer. Peking man probably ate most of his food raw and used the fires primarily for warmth and protection from wild beasts.

In comparison with the achievements of modern man, Peking man's control over nature seems limited and scarcely effective. He must have lived much like the animals he hunted. Presumably he had no houses but used natural shelters such as caves and perhaps crude brush shelters. Yet Peking man had some tremendous advantages over other animals — he knew and controlled fire, and he was not limited by the equipment of his own body but had created tools which permitted him to accomplish tasks otherwise impossible. The fact that he was able to kill elephants, deer, and wild horses shows that he had made a long step toward use of cultural knowledge for survival.

In making a living, Peking man was primarily a predatory hunter of other animals. Nearly all of the hunted animals were more than a match for him physically, and it was Peking man's knowledge of tools, fire, and perhaps traps that gave him the advantage. Probably Peking man also made use of plant foods, such as roots or berries, but no evidence of these has been found, and the quantity of animal bones suggests that Peking man was primarily a meat eater. As a grim note, it should be mentioned that the Peking individuals from Chou Kou Tien were themselves apparently food remains. Peking man subsisted partly (although probably in a minor way) by eating other Peking men. All of the human skulls from Chou Kou Tien have had their basal portions broken out as only man would do; the presumption is that Peking man himself was responsible and that the breakage was to gain access to the brains of the victims.

The carnivorous propensities of Peking man are matter for remark. Of man's animal relatives, the living apes, none are habitual meat eaters. Even the fierce baboons and 600-pound gorillas are vegetarians and depend primarily on plant foods. We do not know when in man's history the eating of meat became important, but it was present among the Australopithecinae and was obviously well established by the time of Peking Man.

From the simplicity of his tools, Peking man could not have been very efficient at exploiting his environment. Although he had an advantage over the animals around him because of his intelligence and his manufactured artifacts, the hunting activities must have been a constant task for the men (and perhaps the women)

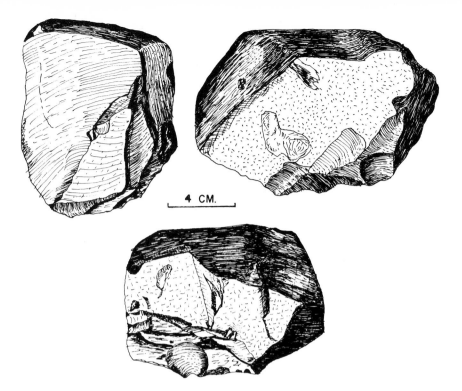

4 CM.

Fig. 13. Rude stone chopping tools from Chou Kou Tien. *These are the characteristic tools associated with Peking man. (Compare Figs. 12 and 14–15.) Redrawn after Davidson Black*, Memoirs of the Geological Survey of China, *Peiping, Ser. A. Vol. 11.*

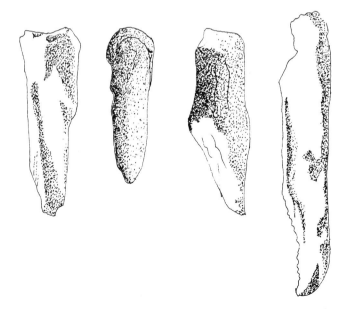

Fig. 14. Fragments of animal bone believed to have been used as tools by Peking man. *The broken pieces, ranging from 3½ to 6 inches long, do not show deliberate shaping but were probably used as fractured. (Compare Figs. 12–13 and 15.) Redrawn after Davidson Black*, Memoirs of the Geological Survey of China, *Peiping, Ser. A, Vol. 11.*

of the group, with frequent periods of famine. There was little leisure for thinking of abstract things like philosophy, religion, or even improvements for the prevailing stone tools. Culture change must have been exceedingly slow under such conditions.

Studies of the brain casts of Peking man have suggested that he had a spoken language and hence could communicate with his fellows far more effectively than animals can. Presumably he lived in groups, but these must have been small and may have been no larger than single families; such a living pattern is common to many other mammals, including gorillas. There is no evidence of a chief or leader, although again by analogy to other animals it seems likely that a large and vigorous individual would have some control or dominance over weaker individuals. There is also no archaeological evidence of cooperative effort, but it is logical to assume that hunting bigger animals such as elephants required the cooperation of a group. It is hard to believe that a single man armed only with a sharp rock could attack an elephant with much prospect of staying alive, let alone killing the animal. If cooperative hunting efforts did take place in this early period of human history, they represent the beginnings of social organization.

There is no art object of any kind in the Peking collection, no adornment of cave walls with paint or scratches, and not even the aesthetic expression of finishing a tool with better workmanship than is necessary for its function. There is no indication of philosophy or religion, games or amusements. Apparently the task of making a living occupied the complete attention of the people, and we find no forerunners of the cultural elaborations prominent in later times. Such lack of self-realization can be partly attributed to the lack of leisure and to the harsh necessities of physical survival, but it may also result from a less developed intelligence and from biological differences between Peking man and later humans. Leisure *permits* the development of the "inner man" but does not *produce* such development. The average domestic cat, for example, has an abundance of leisure, but he does not use it as humans do. In any event, the beginnings of self-realization activities apparently come considerably later in time than the use or manufacture of tools. But not too long after the time of Peking man, evidences of ornament and similar embellishments appear in the archaeological record, and from then on the "finer things of life" have become increasingly important to mankind.

It is not likely that any modern man, even the most "primitive," would enjoy the company of Peking man or see much to admire in him; his animal qualities would be prominently apparent to any contemporary human. We can appreciate Peking man as a possible pioneer of human culture, but it is easier to appreciate such pioneers in retrospect than it might be if we had to live with them.

SELECTED REFERENCES

ANONYMOUS

1959   A "Stupendous Discovery": The Fossil Skull from Olduvai which represents "the oldest well-established toolmaker ever found." *The Illustrated London News*, September 12, 1959, pp. 217, 219. London. The news report announcing the discovery of Zinjanthropus.

BLACK, DAVIDSON, AND OTHERS

1933   Sinanthropus Cultural Remains. *Memoirs of the Geological Survey of China, Peiping*, series A, Vol. II, pp. 110-136. The original description of the stone tools from the Peking man discovery site.

BOULE, MARCELIN, AND H. V. VALLOIS

1957   *Fossil Men.* Dryden, New York. A general work summarizing biological and cultural details for fossil human finds up to 1957.

BREUIL, H.

1939   Bone and Antler Industry of the Choukoutien Sinanthropus Site. *Paleontologica Sinica*, new series, series D, Vol. 6, No. 1. Peiping. A brief article by a French prehistorian describing the bone tools associated with Peking man.

HOWELL, F. C.

1959   The Villafranchian and Human Origins. *Science*, Vol. 130, No. 3379, pp. 831-844. Washington. A summary account of the earliest humans, their geographic distribution and relationships.

LEAKEY, L. S. B.

1959   The Newly-discovered Skull from Olduvai: First Photographs of the Complete Skull. *The Illustrated London News*, September 19, 1959, pp. 288-289. London. News report of the discovery of Zinjanthropus.

1960a   *Adam's Ancestors: The Evolution of Man and His Culture.* Harper, New York. A general work describing human evolution.

1960b   *Olduvai Gorge.* Cambridge University Press, Cambridge. General discussion of Leakey's work and finds made at Olduvai.

VON KOENIGSWALD, G. H. R.

1956   *Meeting Prehistoric Man.* Harper, New York. Written by a scholar who has himself made important discoveries of fossil humans, this popular treatment gives facts about some of the fossil finds and the expeditions which recovered them.

4 UPPER PALEOLITHIC MAN AND HIS DESCENDANTS: The Birth of Art and Agriculture

The limited Lower Paleolithic culture of Peking man was followed by hundreds of thousands of years during which very gradual trends can be discerned (although no continuity can be demonstrated). Then major cultural changes took place perhaps 40,000 years ago. During the long time of the Lower Paleolithic, even the simple technology of incipient cultures gave man advantages over other animals, and as a result the human population of the earth increased and became more widespread. The magnitude of the increase can be but roughly estimated, but judging from the more numerous archaeological sites known for later periods, there must have been a steady increase in man's numbers.

With increase in numbers and expansion of area, the Lower Paleolithic cultures show a tendency toward fragmentation and separation of human groups. As small bands occupied new regions and lost contact with other humans, each group began to develop its own traditions and technology along lines best suited to its own needs, particularly in adapting to new and varied environmental conditions as humans spread out of tropical regions into quite different climate zones. Such cultural differentiation is limited in comparison to that of recent times, but in the assemblages of Lower Paleolithic tools regional patterns of tool making can be distinguished. Southern Africa and southeast Asia largely continued in the tradition of *choppers* and chopping tools, similar to

Fig. 15. **An Acheulean fist ax from Europe.** *Differentiation of tool traditions occurred early in the Lower Paleolithic, and while southern Africa and Asia continued to use the chopper tools like those in Fig. 12 and Fig. 13 (also compare Fig. 12), northern Africa and Europe developed a tool tradition dependent upon using the fist ax like the specimen above. Fist axes are more regular in shape and more carefully made than chopper tools, and while chopper tools are usually made by striking flakes from one surface only, fist axes are made by trimming flakes from both sides of the stone core. The scale is in centimeters. Photograph by M. Kowta.*

those of Peking man. Northern Africa, Europe, and the Near East developed the *fist ax* of the Chellean-Acheulean tradition. Such tools are general-purpose utensils like the choppers of Peking man, but fist axes show more standardized form and workmanship and indicate a step forward in planning technological creations.

Another trend revealed in the finds is a shift from the more primitive human forms toward the physical type of modern man. As has been mentioned, Zinjanthropus is in some ways more like an ape than a man; Peking man is definitely human but still shows a number of primitive biological features. Other intermediate forms are known which are only slightly (but recognizably) different from modern man, the best-known being Neanderthal man (*Homo neanderthalensis*). Neanderthals lived to about 40,000 years ago, well into the time of modern man (*Homo sapiens*). The biological history of man is in itself a fascinating and complex study, but for present purposes only an outline is given to show that man's cultural history is correlated with his biological developments. About 40,000 years ago, *Homo sapiens* became the only surviving form of man, and all subsequent cultural developments can be attributed to humans essentially like those of today. Although many details of the story remain to be worked out, it appears that *Homo neanderthalensis* interbred with *Homo sapiens* in at least some parts of the Near East. Neanderthal man may have been assimilated rather than exterminated by the modern form of human.

Although population increased and the beginnings of cultural diversity appeared during the Lower Paleolithic, the basic life way remained the same. More experience with tools and weapons and probably more effective social cooperation made man the master of the largest beasts, and such animals as the mammoth were systematically procured for food. Yet the people were still hunters and gatherers dependent upon foods provided by nature.

No pronounced changes in social adaptation or self-realization can be seen in the archaeological record until the end of the Lower Paleolithic period. Then Neanderthal man seems to have made the first deliberate burials. Before these, the dead were apparently abandoned and no graves were prepared. The preparation of a grave is significant in marking social concern and presumably some sort of funeral ritual. When the grave is provided with offerings of food and worldly possessions, the inference is that the mourners believed such offerings could be used somehow by the dead person — in other words, that there was a spirit or soul that continued to live. Hence, the beginning of graves, funerals, and burial offerings is usually considered to represent the origin of religion.

Upper Paleolithic cultures, associated with the waning of the glaciers of the Pleistocene or Ice Age, showed many features of increasing culture development. The trends mentioned above continued, with the result that cultures become very diverse and widely scattered. Although the earliest evidences for human development come, as we have seen, from central Africa and southern Asia — tropical and subtropical regions at the time of hominid development — by 20,000 years ago human remains were deposited throughout Europe, Africa, and Asia, and there is some reason to believe that even the New World was beginning to be penetrated by human groups from Asia. The archaeological sites of this period are often mixed, having several successive deposits of cultural and natural materials; the superposition indicates increasing populations and repeated occupations of the same village location. Further, the number of tools and activities of man increased so that the cultural content of remains is more extensive and a single archaeological site is unlikely to suggest the full roster of Upper Paleolithic accomplishments. Ideally, an Upper Paleolithic site would contain evidence of the whole range of culture: burials, grave offerings, paintings, sculptures, and dozens of clearly specialized artifact types, all of these occurring without remains of earlier or later peoples mixed in. Discovery of such a site is a goal of many archaeologists; so far the published record has no single location in which all aspects of an Upper Paleolithic culture are present in clear association. The result is that the paintings tend to be known from one place, graves from another, and specialized tools from still another location.

In sites from the Upper Paleolithic and later times, therefore, it becomes difficult to find a complete cross section of a culture in one place. The examples of excavation given here must be supplemented with data from other finds in order to give a complete picture. A good example of careful scientific investigation is that of the rock shelter at La Colombière in central France, near Poncin.

La Colombière

The site of La Colombière represents a time when man had become proficient as a cultural creature, with a conscious appreciation of what tool manufacture and tool use could do in provision of food. This period, a division of the Upper Paleolithic, is best known from sites in France although sites of the same culture are found widely in Europe. Although he was a hunter, La Colombière man's existence was secure enough so that part of his life could be devoted to social and artistic matters.

Problems of archaeological classification become quite complex for the Upper Paleolithic since there was a great deal more variation in the tools made, and the archaeological sites of different regions show more diversity and complexity than older remains. Archaeologists have attempted to sort out the differences by naming distinctive tool assemblages — these constitute "cultures" in the archaeological sense. The culture of La Colombière belongs to a subdivision of the Upper Paleolithic named *Perigordian* (after an assemblage of stone tools first described from another French site at Périgord). The Perigordian is marked off from other Paleolithic cultures by its distinctive varieties of small stone tools. A developmental sequence can be determined within the Perigordian, and La Colombière is assigned to the later part of it, the *Upper Perigordian*. Such a classification is useful in defining the tool assemblage and in seeking comparative material (other Upper Perigordian sites are known), but it must be realized that these terms are essentially descriptive and technological and that their broader meaning is not clear. Certainly any two sites sharing an Upper Perigordian assemblage of stone tools are related, but the degree and extent of the relationship is not known. The people of such sites *could* be members of the same tribal group with closely similar customs and beliefs. On the other hand, they might be merely sharing common tool traditions from ancestral groups and be very dissimilar in such things as language, religion, "nationality," and physical type. Careful descriptive categories are an essential first step for cultural reconstruction, but archaeological terms like Upper Perigordian cannot be taken to be equivalent in meaning to ethnographic labels like "Eskimo" or "Bantu."

The time of the Upper Perigordian is not yet precisely known. Radiocarbon dates on the order of 15,000 years ago have been determined for samples from the deposits at La Colombière, although scholars who have studied the cave most carefully feel that geological evidence indicates somewhat greater age and that the samples may somehow be contaminated. Such a possibility must always be considered for cultures of this antiquity. The older the site, the more chance that it has been contaminated by charcoal from visits of later peoples. Another Upper Perigordian site at Les Eyzies yielded radiocarbon dates of about 24,000 years ago on charcoal from a hearth. This suggests that the Upper Perigordian deposits at La Colombière may well be somewhat older than the radiocarbon dates from the site, and recent estimates give about 20,000 years as the age for La Colombière. These estimates are supported by geological evidence of glacial deposits representing the final (Würm) glaciation in Europe. The latitude of these estimates is of minor significance in evaluating the amount and direction of human culture change between the time of Peking man and the time of the Upper Perigordian people who were *Homo sapiens*. The age of Peking man is measured in hundreds of thousands of years, and the Upper Perigordian culture represents the advances made by humans during this long time. By the time of Upper Perigordian men, at least 90 per cent of man's cultural history had gone by.

The site of La Colombière is typical of Upper Paleolithic sites in that it is in a cave overlooking a river. Many sites of this kind are known because of man's tendency to use natural shelters adjacent to fresh water. Gravels of the fourth glacial period were deposited by periodic flooding from the adjacent river; these gravels buried the artifacts left by intermittent occupation and provided both a protective blanket for the cultural remains and a means of correlating man's activities with geological periods.

La Colombière is properly a rock shelter — a habitation area below a massive overhanging rock outcrop — rather than a true cave. The sheltered area is about 150 by 30 feet and contained a deposit of about 10 feet of artifact-bearing earth and gravel. The upper layers contained materials attributable to fairly recent times, but these upper deposits are not of concern here and the present discussion involves only the Upper Perigordian materials from the site.

La Colombière was first dug by archaeologists in the 1860's, but even before that time much material from the upper deposits of the shelter had been dug away by farmers. Intermittent digging by relic collectors continued until the first intensive scientific digging was done by Lucien Mayet and Jean Pissot, French archaeologists who excavated at La Colombière for over a year in 1913-1914. Their monograph, published in 1915, reports on the excavation of over a thousand cubic meters from the site. Further investigations were directed by H. L. Movius in 1948 for Harvard University. The Harvard expedition excavated all of the remaining cultural deposit and made detailed studies of the stratigraphy and dating.

Fig. 16. The site of La Colombière, France. *The shelter can be seen just left of the center with the pile of excavated earth at its mouth. Reproduced by permission of H. L. Movius and Hugh Hencken from Movius and Judson (1956).*

Fig. 17. Excavation at the site of La Colombière. *Reproduced by permission of H. L. Movius and Hugh Hencken from Movius and Judson (1956).*

The collections from the 1914 French excavations were restudied by Movius in combination with specimens found in his own work, and information from the two studies is combined to give a summary of the total contents of the Perigordian layers of the site. The artifact finds included:

1361 flint implements (plus several thousand chips and flakes resulting from flint-chipping activities)

38 bone and antler objects and one ivory artifact

2 engraved mammoth bones

10 engraved pebbles bearing several superimposed drawings of different animals

2 beads, one piece of red ocher, and several perforated shells collected by inhabitants of the site and drilled for suspension as ornaments

In addition to the artifacts, several thousand animal bones were found, providing information on food resources and the climate of the time.

No burials of the Upper Perigordian people were found, but from finds in other sites it is known that the people buried their dead in prepared graves, often providing offerings. Although no paintings were found, other sites of the time had paintings on cave walls.

At first glance the inventory looks not too different from the sort of thing found in Peking man's cave at Chou Kou Tien, but a closer look shows many significant differences. The stone tools at La Colombière, despite their apparent simplicity, are not randomly battered rocks but patterned implements of several kinds, made to perform specific functions and produced according to standardized manufacturing techniques. Where Peking man had only a generalized idea for his stone tools, the dwellers at La Colombière knew how to utilize specific qualities of their materials. They could produce small delicate tools for engraving, heavy-duty tools for cutting or scraping, shaped points for boring holes, and similar specialized devices. Where Peking Man took a fist-sized rock and trimmed it into an implement, Upper Perigordian man attained his ends by using a flake off the rock rather than the mass of the stone itself. This distinction between Lower and Upper Paleolithic cultures is fundamental; the latter in general used less material and made lighter, sharper, more easily produced stone tools. The difference is clearly in the direction of greater technological sophistication, and although the tools of La Colombière appear crude by modern standards, they are well advanced beyond the beginnings of human tool use.

Better knowledge and use of tools is also seen in the bone tools from La Colombière. These tend to be shaped all over and they show control of grinding processes (as well as the chipping used in stone working). Instead of the random questionable pieces of broken bone from Peking man's tool kit, La Colombière specimens, simple though they are, are clearly conceived and well-manufactured tools. Also noteworthy are bone implements that bear decoration in the form of parallel engraved lines. These lines have no effect on the use of the bone tool and are, therefore, significant as indicators that La Colombière man placed a conscious value on his technology. It was no longer enough to have any crude tool that would work; man now wanted a good functional tool that not only did the job but also had some satisfying quality of form or decoration independent of the tool's use. This simple kind of decoration is the first tangible evidence of a "sense of elegance" — a feeling that not only is there a job to be done, but that there is a pleasing way of doing it that is worth extra effort.

Despite these clear improvements in technology, the people of La Colombière still gained their livelihood from hunting large game animals, as Peking man had done thousands of years previously. The animal remains from La Colombière included many of the same kinds of animals: wild boar, a type of large deer, rhinoceros, wild horse, and mammoth. The commonest animal at La Colombière was a reindeer (*Rangifer tarandus*). Presumably, the people of La Colombière were somewhat more efficient than Peking man in securing large food animals, and therefore life at La Colombière was probably relatively free of famine and threat of famine. Direct evidence for such a conclusion depends upon quantitative analyses of the faunal remains, and comparative studies of this kind have not been done for the sites in question. However, indirect evidence for a higher living standard in the Upper Perigordian is convincing and several indications can be mentioned: improved technology, larger population, and the evidences of leisure reflected in art and decorative ornament.

The relationships of the people at La Colombière to one another are also difficult to infer from the archaeology. So far as

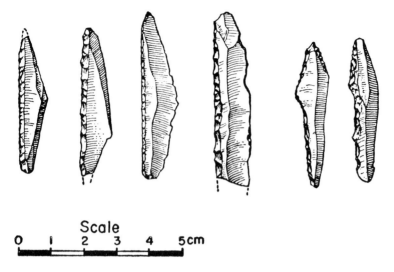

Scale

0   1   2   3   4   5cm

Fig. 18. Backed blades from the Perigordian levels of La Colombière. *Such tools show the increasing specialization of tools in the Upper Paleolithic. These are made from precisely detached flakes of flint only an inch or two long and serve as cutting tools. As struck from the flint core, these small longitudinal flakes have razor-sharp edges. In order to use them without cutting the fingers, one edge (the back) is blunted by chipping it so that a dull surface is provided for finger pressure. Reproduced by permission of H. L. Movius and Hugh Hencken from Movius and Judson (1956).*

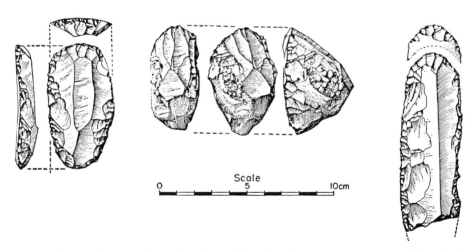

Scale
0   5   10cm

Fig. 19. Scrapers from La Colombière. *Stone tools of the Perigordian (and the Upper Paleolithic in general) show a much advanced conception and knowledge of tool making. Compared to the earlier Lower Paleolithic stone tools, these are smaller, lighter, more patterned in form, and made of flakes struck from a piece of flint rather than the central core of flint. Reproduced by permission of H. L. Movius and Hugh Hencken from Movius and Judson (1956).*

64

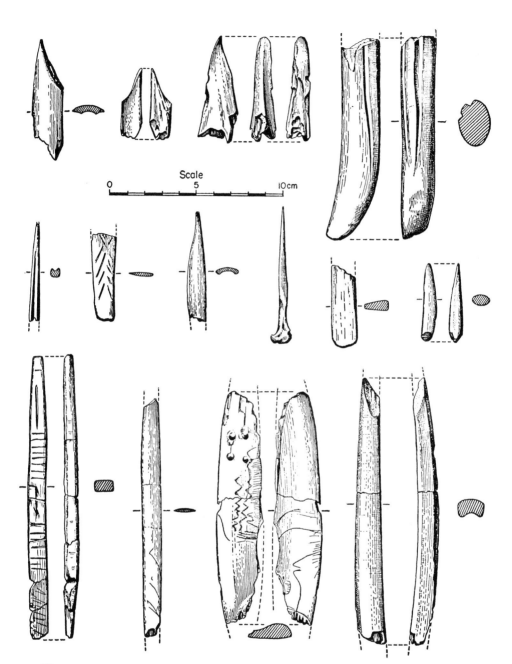

Fig. 20. Bone and antler implements from La Colombière. *Sites of the Upper Paleolithic reveal the first use of carefully shaped and polished bone tools and indicate the expansion of man's technology from reliance on chipped stone tools. Note also that some of these items bear incised ornamentation showing that the makers wished their tools to be aesthetically pleasing as well as functional. Such indications are absent in the tool assemblages of the Lower Paleolithic. (Compare Fig. 70.) Reproduced by permission of H. L. Movius and Hugh Hencken from Movius and Judson (1956).*

65

can be told, the people of La Colombière lived (like Peking man) in family groups with a minimum of community or tribal organization. The sites of the time do not represent towns or even villages but rather seasonal stopping places inhabited by limited numbers of people. Even so, there must have been many more people than in earlier times, for Upper Paleolithic sites are more numerous than Lower Paleolithic locations.

There is little evidence that some individuals of Perigordian communities were marked off from the bulk of the population by virtue of wealth or social status as chiefs or rulers. Yet there is reason to believe that at least two kinds of people were important and had positions of influence in the community, if not formal offices. In all hunting communities of primitives in our own times, the skilled and successful hunter is an admired and respected person; it is a safe inference that the people of La Colombière looked up to their outstanding hunters in the same way. Such a man may not be a chief in the sense that he has political power to direct others and yet his personal influence can be very great — he is marked off from others by his successful accomplishments of valued goals.

A second category of important people among present-day hunting groups comprises magicians or people believed to have ritual powers permitting them to influence nature and the welfare of the group. Such persons, often called *shamans,* are important to the community because (it is thought) they have powers beyond the scope of the ordinary man. Before Neanderthal man, it is doubtful whether humans had so conceived of nature and spiritual power as to permit the idea of a shaman. By the time of La Colombière, however, the practice of intentional burial of the dead was well established and the idea of spirits and superhuman powers must have been present. The development of artistic representation in the Upper Paleolithic (shown by the engraved pebbles and bones at La Colombière and by the contemporary cave paintings from other locations in France) has been equated by many scholars with hunting magic, and it is frequently proposed that the artists of Upper Paleolithic times were in fact shamans whose artistic productions had magical significance. Such a conclusion cannot be proven, but it seems plausible on comparative grounds for several reasons: the engraved pieces from La Colombière show only animals; they were not made to be viewed as art objects (or else there would not be several pictures scratched one on top of the other so that the images are obscured) ; and they occur together in groups. All these facts suggest that the act of making the image was important, not the finished product. And since the images are of the large animals so important to existence, it is reasonable to conclude that the art practices were connected with shamanism in some way.

Whether the artists of La Colombière were shamans or not, they were probably people recognized by their social group as individuals of special ability. Much artistic skill is necessary to produce such drawings. Although simple, the engravings of animals are realistic in proportion and appearance and are good enough representations to make it easy to recognize what animal was intended. Not everyone in a society (including our own) has the observational or motor skills to make such a drawing and few contemporary people can imitate the cave paintings accurately. The talent of drawing, recognized as a special ability in the modern world, must have been impressive to the hunters of La Colombière, in whose lives any kind of representational art was exceedingly rare.

The significance of evidence for incipient "chiefs" and "shamans" at La Colombière is in showing the first real differentiation based on social or cultural factors. Preceding peoples had differentiation based on age and sex, and on dominance of strong over weak individuals, but such distinctions are based on biological rather than cultural factors. The emergence of capable hunters as important people reflects a valuing of cultural knowledge, since the successful hunter attains his goals through skill in making and using weapons rather than through physical qualities alone. Whatever role the artists of La Colombière played was probably affected by their cultural skill and the admiration or awe of less talented individuals. Such biologically determined features as age and sex continue to have importance, but man from the time of La Colombière, if not before, has superimposed social and cultural values on the biological base. Such social and cultural factors are often more important to humans than the physical ones. Social differentiation such as that based on age and sex has always been present and is found among apes, monkeys, and many animals very different from man. Social differentiation depending upon social and cultural knowledge, however, is much more recent in

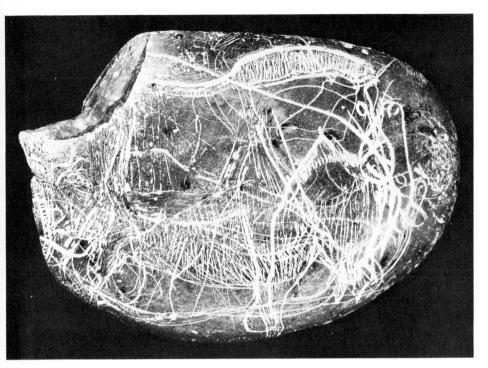

Fig. 21. One of the engraved pebbles from La Colombière. *The photo shows the numerous superimposed engravings on the pebble; the drawing, one of the figures portrayed, a wild horse. The maximum length is 12 cm. This is the obverse side; see Fig. 22 for the reverse. Reproduced by permission of H. L. Movius and Hugh Hencken from Movius and Judson (1956).*

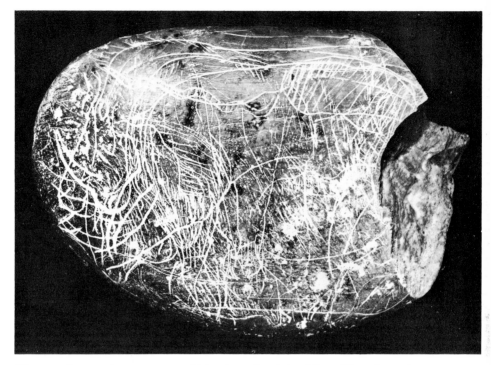

Fig. 22. One of the engraved pebbles from La Colombière. *The photo shows the number of superimposed engravings on the pebble; the drawing, one of the figures portrayed, a woolly rhinoceros. This is the reverse side of the pebble shown in Fig. 21. Reproduced by permission of H. L. Movius and Hugh Hencken from Movius and Judson (1956).*

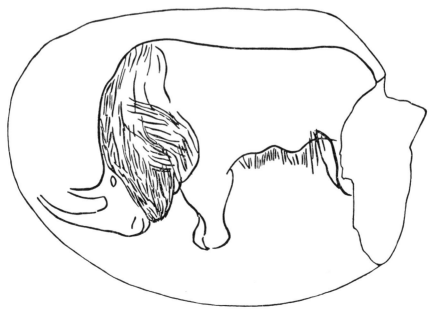

human history and La Colombière's few tantalizing clues are among the oldest indications.

The finds at La Colombière also show the beginnings of a striving to satisfy the "inner man." The earlier periods of the Lower Paleolithic have left nothing in the archaeological record to support the old saying that "man does not live by bread alone." It appears rather that he did live only for satisfaction of his physical needs. But the people of La Colombière seem to have felt the need for additional things in life, as shown by their art work and evidence of personal adornment.

The art of the engraved animals may in its inception have been purely functional, serving only magical purposes. Yet it soon came also to have aesthetic meaning, if not in the phase represented by La Colombière, then certainly by the end of the Upper Paleolithic. The decoration of tools (as by the scratching of lines on bone objects) may also have a function, perhaps to increase the efficiency of the tools by magical means, perhaps simply to represent "maker's marks" so that the owner could recognize his own manufactures. Yet these too, whatever their functional import, also satisfy man's urge for attractive as well as useful objects. The La Colombière collection also includes some perforated shells, presumably for personal adornment — further indications of aesthetic interests. Finally, the lump of red ocher indicates that something (probably man himself) was being decorated with this very common natural pigment. All in all, La Colombière provided a fair roster of such finds in comparison with sites like that of Peking man, where nothing was recovered to which this kind of interpretation can be applied.

A sense of powers beyond those of man (religion in the broadest sense) is seen in the suggestions of shamanism and the custom of burial, well established by the time of La Colombière. We can assume that man of this time was conscious of a need to understand, and if possible control, the forces that affected his destiny. The search for satisfactory explanations of nature and the phenomena of life and death had probably begun before the time of La Colombière. Unfortunately, however, there is no way to reconstruct this part of man's development in detail. Archaeology cannot provide more than a meager outline of Upper Paleolithic developments of this kind.

Within a few thousand years after the Upper Perigordian occupation of La Colombière, the developments revealed there in incipient form flourished as the descendants of the Upper Perigordian man improved and expanded upon their inherited knowledge. Art in particular developed to a degree that inspires respect even from modern man; and later culture groups, particularly those of the Magdalenian culture, produced elaborate polychrome cave paintings of animals. In the technology, the number, variety, and decoration of bone implements increased rapidly, to the point where some Upper Paleolithic collections (from the latest periods) contain more bone implements than stone ones.

The Upper Paleolithic is best known for the appearance of art as a part of human life. Yet many other significant developments also took place during this time, including a variety of technological improvements of some importance. Not only did these changes lay the groundwork for the improvements of succeeding eras, but they also show that men of this time were fully familiar with, interested in, and dependent upon, the making and using of a variety of tools. For the rude near-men, and largely for the whole of the Lower Paleolithic, tool using is almost an incidental part of human life, important to be sure but in no sense a characteristic and vital part of humanity. From the time of Upper Paleolithic man to the present day, however, it is not possible to consider human life without recognizing the important role played by technology. Four of the key developments that have been pointed out for the Upper Paleolithic include the following:

1. Grinding and polishing as a tool-making method, in addition to the chipping and pounding techniques of all earlier humans. Development of grinding and polishing methods had several values for Upper Paleolithic man: it made available to him a large number of raw materials (such as bone) which are not very amenable to the older chipping or hammering methods; and it permitted the development of a wide range of forms not feasible through a chipping technique alone. Grinding techniques also reflect greater patience and foresight in tool making, since the average chipped object can be made in minutes while the average ground object usually requires hours of manufacturing time. Upper Paleolithic man applied grinding and polishing techniques primarily to bone and ivory materials, and it is not until the later Neolithic period that polished objects of stone (such as axes) are found.

2. The spear thrower, a bone or wood device held in the hand and used to propel spears, was invented in the Upper Paleolithic. This device in effect lengthens the throwing arm of the hunter, permitting him a much more forceful propulsion of his weapon. The invention greatly improved the effectiveness of the hunter against the big game animals of the Upper Paleolithic. Such animals as reindeer, elephants, and horses are not apt to be disabled by a hunter throwing rocks at them, but a spear thrown from a spear thrower is much more damaging. It is not inconceivable that the invention of the spear thrower played a large part in the extinction of many of the large Pleistocene animals, so great an advantage does this device give the human hunter. Use of the spear thrower has continued until recent times among such groups as the Eskimo (Fig. 23).

3. The Upper Paleolithic has also been noted as having a considerable number of tools used to make other tools. Among these is the shaft wrench, a perforated bone or antler object used as a lever to straighten the light wooden or cane shafts of spears and arrows. This tool is a manufacturing device and not something that is used directly in obtaining food. It is, like the spear thrower, an implement persisting into recent times — one not unlike Upper Paleolithic specimens was recovered from a sixteenth-century site in California (Fig. 70).

    Also in the category of tools used to make tools are many of the small and specialized flint tools among those from La Colombière; many of these tools apparently had as their purpose the shaping or engraving of wood and bone.

4. The beginnings of compound tools — tools made of two or more parts — must lie in the Upper Paleolithic. In the succeeding Mesolithic period, as mentioned below, compound tools become dominant, but even in the Upper Paleolithic some compound devices must have been used. An example is the harpoon or fish spear with a barbed bone point and a wooden shaft.

All of these innovations taken together show that man of the Upper Paleolithic had improved in quite significant ways on the more limited technology of the previous humans to develop a more adaptable, more flexible, and more specialized array of tools. Certainly this array must have improved man's ability to exploit the resources of his environment.

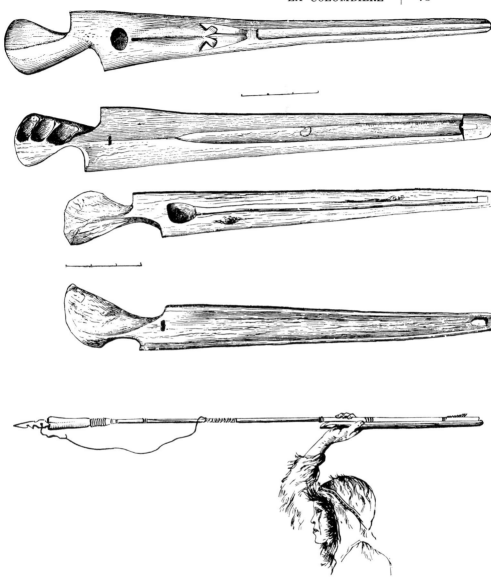

Fig. 23. Recent Eskimo spear throwers of wood. *Length about 19 inches. The spear thrower was an invention of the Upper Paleolithic that greatly increased man's weapon power, enabling him to throw small spears with much greater force than is possible with his unaided arm. These devices continued in use until recent times, providing ethnographic analogies for interpreting the archaeological specimens. The spear rests in a longitudinal groove, butt against a stop at the narrow rearward end. The grip is at the broad forward end. As the throw begins, one or more fingers keep the spear in the groove; when they release the spear, the butt rest of the thrower continues to drive the spear, in effect lengthening the user's arm and increasing the launch speed. Reprinted by permission of the United States National Museum.*

THE MESOLITHIC

In Europe, the developments of the Upper Paleolithic come to an end between about 12,000 and 15,000 years ago with the onset of changing environmental conditions. The last ice sheets of northern Europe melted away, the climate of Europe became somewhat warmer, and many of the large animals hunted by Upper Paleolithic man became extinct. Man may have played a part in the extinction of the larger animals, since his improving technology gave him an ever-increasing advantage over the animals and at the same time his increasing population demanded more and more food. Whatever the cause, it is clear that the way of life appropriate to the people of the Upper Paleolithic did not continue; the archaeological record shows a shift to new resources.

The shift marks the beginning of the *Mesolithic* (middle stone) period, a time marked most prominently by the development of settled villages along lakes, streams, and ocean shores. The villages were supported by hunting and gathering, but hunting and gathering of more generalized nature, apparently, than that practiced in the Paleolithic. Upper Paleolithic peoples such as those at La Colombière were rather specialized hunters, according to the animal bones in the site. These hunters utilized such large animals as reindeer and seldom turned to such smaller creatures as rabbits. Mesolithic peoples made much greater use of shellfish and marine resources as well as smaller animals; they may also have expanded their use of plant foods.

The Mesolithic is viewed by some scholars as a cultural decline, a sort of "dark age" during which man stood still or lost some of his previous cultural knowledge, principally because the impressive art of the Upper Paleolithic disappeared. Perhaps there was no longer any need for such magicoreligious paintings, with the large animals mostly gone and the way of life shifting to use of less imposing food resources. However, while Mesolithic peoples had little to offer of artistic endeavor (at least of art that survived) it would be a mistake to conclude that their culture declined to the extent that people were worse off than they had been before. On the contrary, population apparently increased through the Mesolithic, showing that man maintained or improved his capability for survival. Also, some of the technological trends continued. For example, Mesolithic man continued to make his stone tools smaller and lighter and reached a point of using very small stone flakes imbedded in wooden or bone handles as knives or cutting instruments. Such tiny stone flakes are not impressive archaeological finds, but they represent an increasing refinement of technology in that man had reached a clear understanding that his objective in many tools is a sharp edge. He therefore reduced the weight and bulk of his tools as much as possible while still retaining the sharpness and hardness of edge provided by flint or other stone. Also, he showed sophistication in that he produced compound tools, that is, *stone* flakes set in *wooden* handles, to utilize one material for one set of physical qualities and another material for a different set of properties.

Peoples of generalized mesolithic culture have existed in all parts of the world until near contemporary times. Thousands of archaeological sites give good pictures of the Mesolithic way of life, some of the sites as recent as a few hundred years ago. One of the culture sites of mesolithic type is the Drakes Bay village discussed in Chapter 7.

THE NEOLITHIC

Somewhere in the several thousand years during which Mesolithic cultures were dominant, there occurred one of the most significant changes ever brought about by man, namely the development of *producing* food by domestication of plants and animals. When this change took place, man ceased being dependent entirely on what he could find in nature and achieved some control over his food resources by starting to keep and breed plants and animals.

The change to food production marks the beginning of a cultural phase labeled *Neolithic* (new stone), originally so named because of the introduction at this time of polished or ground stone tools. It was soon found, however, that the more significant development of the time was in the change from hunting and gathering to domestication of plants and animals. This change has often been referred to as the *Neolithic revolution* because of its revolutionary effect on the life of man. The revolution was not abrupt; the shift from wild plants and animals to those bred by man occupied a minimum of two or three thousand years in both the Old World and the New World.

The development of agriculture in the Old World took place somewhere in the Near East; the first agriculture may have been as early as 7000 or 8000 B.C., but slightly later sites provide the earliest firm evidence. In the New World, the time and place of agricultural origins are less well known, but the beginnings are presumed to be somewhere in Central or South America and probably a couple of thousand years later than in the Old World. Indeed, for substantial areas of the world the domestication of animals and the use of agriculture are even more recent. Many cultural groups never experienced the Neolithic revolution at all, but persisted as hunters and gatherers until they were overwhelmed or absorbed by other peoples. These overtaken groups include the Australian Aborigines, the Bushmen of Africa, and many of the American Indian tribes.

One of the difficulties in studying this important shift to food production is that a people beginning a farming way of life or making the first steps at plant and animal domestication leaves little in the archaeological record to mark the change from hunting and gathering. In the beginning, the tools and weapons of the people are the same as those of hunter-gatherers, so no distinctive artifacts mark the change to domestication. By the time such distinctive implements as plows appear in the archaeological record, agriculture is thousands of years beyond its beginnings. Also, at the start of the change, there are no differences between the wild plants and animals collected from nature and those domesticated by man; again, some time elapses before clearly domesticated kinds of plants and animals are recognizable to archaeologists through physical differences in animal bones and preserved plant parts. Finally, there is no complete abrupt change in which a group of people make their living by hunting on one day and by agriculture the next. Rather, over a long period people get part of their subsistence from their knowledge of hunting and gathering, and part from the increased food available through limited use of domestication. Many recent groups of primitive people, including some American Indians, continued this mixed kind of subsistence until their tribal cultures were broken up by the coming of white settlers.

From these considerations, it is apparent that one of the most difficult things for the archaeologist to recognize is the *incipient* development of plant and animal domestication. Several of the world's leading archaeologists are actively searching for the beginning point in plant and animal domestication; so far, the best conclusion that has been reached for this beginning point is somewhere in the Near East, some time around 7000 or 8000 B.C. The causes for the change are also of great interest, but it is more difficult to find the causes than it is to see the effects. For our next examples attention is turned to fully developed agricultural communities; the marked contrasts between these communities and the simple hunter-gatherer examples are largely due to the enriched life made possible when a stable food supply is ensured by agriculture.

SELECTED REFERENCES

CLARK, J. G. D.
   1952   *Prehistoric Europe: The Economic Basis.* Methuen, London. An excellent detailed treatment of the adaptation to environment of the prehistoric peoples of Europe. Gives the evidence for the early hunting and gathering techniques practiced by prehistoric man.

MAYET, LUCIEN, AND JEAN PISSOT
   1915   Abri-sous-Roche préhistorique de la Colombière, près Poncin. *Annales de l'Université de Lyon,* Ser. 1, Vol. 39. The original report on La Colombière. Much of the information is included in the later report of Movius and Judson below.

MOVIUS, HALLAM L., AND SHELDON JUDSON
   1956   *The Rock Shelter of La Colombière.* American School of Prehistoric Research, Bulletin 19, Peabody Museum, Harvard University. The site report on which the discussion of La Colombière in this book is based.

TAX, SOL, editor
   1960   *Evolution after Darwin, Vol. II: The Evolution of Man.* University of Chicago Press. A series of essays dealing with biological and cultural evolution and the relationships between them.

WASHBURN, S. L., editor
   1961   *Social Life of Early Man.* Viking Fund Publications in Anthropology No. 31. New York. Eighteen essays which present evidence, conclusions, and hypotheses on the evolution and development of society. Includes discussion of subhuman primate social behavior.

5 UR:
A Bronze Age City

As we have seen, the recognition of incipient agriculture in archaeological remains is most difficult, since there is usually a long period during which early farming communities continue to draw much of their subsistence from hunting and gathering of wild products. An example of such a village of hunter-farmers is given in Chapter 9, which discusses the site of Paragonah, Utah.

Here we turn to one of the early cities where the potential of a food-producing economy was fully realized: the ancient city of Ur, the site of which is in modern Iraq. The site of Ur is 220 miles south of the modern city of Baghdad, on the alluvial plain of the Euphrates Valley, now 160 miles from the Persian Gulf. The area had a flourishing agriculture in ancient times but is now desolate. The site of Ur was discovered in 1852. The following year J. E. Taylor, the British consul at Basrah, found inscribed cylinders at the site, bearing the name of Nabonidus, the last king of Babylon, and also giving the name of the city. Intermittent excavations followed, with a major campaign of excavation begun in 1922 under the direction of the British archaeologist C. Leonard Woolley. This work, done jointly by the British Museum and the Museum of the University of Pennsylvania, occupied twelve seasons, until 1934.

An impressive set of published reports has resulted from study of the site, including many monographs and several books for the general reader. The wealth of information available from Ur and sites of other ancient cities is in marked contrast to the examples discussed heretofore, in which small collections of limited kinds of objects are the rule. The genesis of cities marks an explosive increase in the quantity and diversity of materials available for archaeological study. There are several reasons for this increase.

The migratory community which stays in one place for only a short time leaves scanty amounts of physical debris and hence few and scattered objects for the archaeologist to find. A fixed community piles up mountains of debris from building and rebuilding and from the ordinary accumulation of refuse, cast-off and worn objects, and in general the sort of thing that finds its way to the city dump. For ancient cities the dump may be the streets, yards, and abandoned rooms or buildings; even our modern cities would be gradually buried in junk and garbage (like many ancient cities) if complex and expensive systems of disposal were not maintained.

Sedentary life also leads to proliferation and elaboration of material manufactures. Peoples who are constantly on the move must concentrate their manufacturing activities on objects that can be carried with them. They have neither the time nor the inclination to produce things so complex as buildings or elaborate monuments.

In towns and cities, there is a year-round occupation, and there are more people in one place than in hunting-gathering communities. The more people there are, the more things will be made, used, and eventually discarded. The excavator of a site like La Colombière expects to find a few hundred or a few thousand items to analyze; the excavator of a site like Ur will find his enumeration of individual specimens totaling in the hundreds of thousands, and if the site were completely excavated the number of objects recovered would be counted in millions. Finally, cities can exist only with a much greater and more assured food supply than villages require. To insure such great quantities of food, it is essential to have a relatively advanced technology and social organization to produce, harvest, store, and distribute the crops. Hence, the archaeological remains of any city will yield material remains reflecting this level of development. It is impossible for hunters and gatherers to develop a city and it is impossible for a city to exist with a hunting and gathering technology and social organization. There are no cities in the Stone Age and no Stone Age cultures in the remains of cities.

The differences between sites like Ur and such simpler remains as La Colombière are at first glance so great that there seems little relationship between archaeological studies of the two places. Yet the basic adaptations discussed in Chapter 1 were as essential to the city dwellers of Ur as they were to the cave dwellers of La Colombière. The archaeologist can ask the same basic questions about the remains from both places, and the differing answers measure the development of man's cultural achievements.

The ancient city of Ur was deserted for 2,000 years with nothing to indicate its existence except a series of earth mounds in a desert plain, dominated by a large conical ruin which was once the chief temple of the city. Its streets buried, its walls fallen, visited only by an occasional nomad, the ancient city shows none of its former importance. Yet this is one of the oldest cities in the world; founded as a village in the mudflats of the Euphrates River about 5000 B.C., Ur began as a Neolithic village shortly after the invention of agriculture and continued through all the cultural developments until the time of the Greco-Roman empires. By about 2000 B.C., the time of the Old Testament prophets, Ur had a population of perhaps 300,000 and ranked as one of the major cities of the world. Among Ur's distinguished inhabitants is believed to have been the prophet Abraham. In its long history, Ur was ruled by unknown prehistoric peoples, as well as by Sumerians, Akkadians, Assyrians, and Persians before its abandonment about 400 B.C.

The history of ancient civilization is entombed in the many layers of construction in the deep mounds of Ur. The people of Ur were among the first to use the invention of writing, and the later phases of the city's life are documented by inscriptions and clay tablets. The historic period of Ur begins with the first dynasty, generally set at 2650 B.C. From this time on, documentary sources are available to supplement the archaeological remains. Around 2650 B.C., Ur was the capital of the Sumerians and the chief city-state in Mesopotamia.

We are not here concerned with the times of Ur's greatness. Rather, out of its 5,000-year history let us look at that time, about 2800 to 2600 B.C., when Ur was developing into a powerful city. Agriculture was flourishing in the rich alluvial plain, bronze was in common use, writing had been introduced not long before, and the population was part of the Sumerian group. The original village of Neolithic farmers had grown into a city of Bronze Age civilization.

TABLE 3. CHRONOLOGY OF UR AND SOUTHERN MESOPOTAMIA
(YEARS B.C.)

Details are not agreed. This chart presents a composite drawn from a number of recent scholars' works on the Near East.

Years B.C.	Peoples	Period	Age	Event
400	Assyrians	↑	Iron Age →←	Achaemenian Persians—Ur abandoned as a city.
1750				Hammurabi's Code (at Babylon).
2000	Babylonians	Historic ↑		The prophet Abraham is believed to have lived at Ur.
2123				Third dynasty of Ur, beginning with King Ur Nammu. Major construction of the Ur ziggurat.
2220	Akkadians		Bronze Age	End of Akkadian rule.
2400	Sumerians ↓			End of second dynasty of Ur; Sargon of Akkad rules.
2650		↑ Prehistoric ↓	↓	Beginning of the first dynasty of Ur; beginning of the historic period. The Royal Cemetery. Introduction of writing.
5000			Neolithic ↑	Beginning of the Ubaid period; founding of Ur.
8000 (?)				First beginning of agriculture.

This period is the time of Ur's royal tombs, archaeologically referred to as Early Dynastic, since there were royal families although they are not documented historically in the way characteristic of later dynastic rulers. The royal tombs are important not only for the elaborate and artistic objects found but also because they provide the greatest detail on the technology, social customs, and religious activities of the people. Here, as in many areas of the world, graves are primary sources of information for cultural reconstruction. Excavation of dwellings often yields only broken and discarded objects, but the tombs of important people contain intact specimens of many kinds.

The exact extent of the city at this early time is not known, nor can its population be accurately estimated. The 2,000 years of occupation that followed completely buried the town associated with the royal tombs, and most of the knowledge comes from the excavation of a single extensive cemetery with more than a thousand graves plus sixteen royal tombs. However, enough is known to indicate that even at the time of the royal tombs the city of Ur stood as an elevated mound with city walls and temples projecting above the flat plain of the river. It was surrounded by flat farm land, crisscrossed by canals carrying irrigation waters from the Euphrates River to the fields. In the surrounding country were scattered hamlets, from which farmers came to do their marketing, attend religious ceremonies, pay their taxes, and enjoy the pleasures of a visit to the city.

The extent of the community and the size of its cemetery indicate that the population should be estimated in thousands rather than hundreds — small by modern standards but much greater in size than any of the communities discussed so far in this book, and certainly large enough to classify Ur as a true city. The fact that Ur was no longer a village is clear evidence of the results of food-producing activities. A city of even a few thousand represents more people than can be supported in one place without developed agriculture, and Ur must have had an effective agriculture supporting a level of material prosperity far greater than that of previous peoples. Instead of leading a migratory existence in search of game or of food plants, the people of Ur lived in the same place for generations. Enough food was produced to last from one harvest to the next, and there was a surplus to devote to the welfare of the community. A man not only could accumulate enough food for himself and his family, but could become wealthy with abundant material possessions by building up reserves.

Of the many important discoveries made during the twelve years of excavation at Ur, three aspects of the research are most significant for our purposes. These include the remains of the city itself, the finds from the Royal Cemetery, and the development of writing and its effect on early civilization.

THE REMAINS OF THE CITY

Excavation of Ur revealed dwellings, temples, a surrounding wall (77 feet thick at the base!), and a ziggurat or temple mound. The ziggurat at Babylon, destroyed long ago, has been identified with the Tower of Babel in biblical tradition. The ziggurat at Ur, slightly smaller than the one at Babylon, is the best preserved of the large structures of this type.

Because of the very long time span during which Ur was occupied the city underwent many changes in layout and construction, and most of the prominent features referred to above are known in their final or developed form rather than in that of the early period of the royal tombs. Yet some features seem to have been fairly constant; throughout its life Ur was typified by mudbrick architecture, ranging from simple one-room dwellings for the poorer classes to vaulted tombs, many-roomed palaces, and temples. Of the temples, the chief temple mound or ziggurat is of particular interest.

The ziggurat is a common feature of Sumerian cities, being the largest and highest temple, built on a foundation platform as big and as high as community resources could provide. The ziggurat at Ur was built in several stages, the most recent additions having been made by Nabonidus about 550 B.C. According to inscriptions left by Nabonidus, the ziggurat was founded by Ur Nammu and his son, first kings of the third dynasty of Ur (about 2100 B.C.). Excavation showed that Ur Nammu was chiefly responsible for the construction, since most of the bricks bore his name stamped upon them. However, beneath the Ur Nammu construction, Woolley found another ziggurat, built in a different kind of brickwork, which he dates to the second dynasty. Only small parts of this monument were dug because to excavate it would destroy the bigger monument on top. Therefore, the heart of the second-dynasty ziggurat is still largely unknown, but it is not unlikely that the original foundations were laid during the first dynasty or possibly even during the period of the royal tombs.

The fact that the royal tombs are adjacent to the ziggurat suggests that some central temple existed there at the same time, for in ancient times the graves of rulers were often in or adjacent to the principal religious edifice. The temple at Ur contemporaneous with the royal tombs could still exist buried under the ziggurats of later times, or it could have been destroyed in the process of later enlargement of the temple mound. We can have a reasonable idea of what the temple was like, however, by comparison with the site of Uruk, a contemporaneous city not far away on the opposite bank of the Euphrates. At Uruk, a temple some two or three hundred years older than the time of the royal tombs was studied in detail. This structure, the so-called White Temple of Uruk, was like later ziggurats in consisting of an elevated mud-brick platform (40 feet high) with a mud-brick temple on top, reached by stairs and a ramp up the platform. The temple had a whitewashed exterior and must have been visible for miles in the surrounding flatlands.

We can assume that the occupants of the royal tombs had built and worshiped at a temple somewhat like the White Temple of Uruk. Though such a structure is smaller and less impressive than the ziggurats of later times, it is a not inconsiderable project of design and construction. The rulers of Ur were clearly able to command great labor resources and to direct community effort in the construction of the city walls, the temples, and the elaborate royal tombs themselves.

But as in most cities, the bulk of the building went into housing for the people, arranged along narrow streets and laid out in something comparable to the city blocks of modern times. The common people lived in simple mud-brick houses, small and usually of only one room. Indeed, the residential parts of Ur apparently differed little in appearance from many Near Eastern towns that retain similar housing in the present day.

THE ROYAL CEMETERY

The excavations revealed an extensive cemetery adjacent to the walled enclosure containing the ziggurat. First used about 3000 B.C., just before the first dynasty, the cemetery was also used in later periods, but most of the tombs were somewhat disturbed by repeated digging, construction of buildings at various times, and treasure hunting or grave robbing in prehistoric times.

Over a thousand graves were recorded. Sixteen were royal tombs; the rest were graves of private citizens dug as close as possible to the resting places of their rulers. The common people were buried in simple coffins containing offerings for use in the afterlife, usually food vessels of pottery, weapons, and personal adornments. These graves give much information about the material equipment of the common people, but the royal tombs were far more spectacular, not only in the yield of elaborate material objects but also in providing a detailed picture of social classes.

The sixteen royal tombs each had individual features of interest, and they show considerable architectural diversity and sophistication. Materials of the tomb chambers included mud brick, fired and unfired, and some stones. The use of arches, domes, and vaults shows the skill of the builders. First, a large square pit was dug, entered by a sloping ramp or roadway. In the pit was built a tomb of stone or brick, sometimes a single room and sometimes three or four rooms. The body lay in state on a bier inside the tomb chamber, surrounded by offerings. The funeral involved the ritual killing of servants and retainers who thus joined their master in death to continue serving him in the afterworld. One or two intimate servants were killed before the tomb chamber was sealed up; the remainder died outside the tomb and were buried in the large pit containing the tomb structure. How these people died is not known, but there is no evidence of violence, and the different groups are arranged as they were in life: grooms, musicians, soldiers, even four-wheeled chariots with their draft oxen. One tomb contained 63 sacrificed persons; another royal tomb had the skeletons of 74 retainers.

Only the royal graves contained a constructed tomb chamber and sacrificed humans. From the differences between the graves of commoner and noble, there must have been a great social distance between the common people and the rulers, with the latter taking on the appearance of exalted and divine beings. This elevation of some of the people to high class represents a dramatic change from the situation in hunter-gatherer groups like those of the Upper Paleolithic period. Among the latter, there were probably important men who were respected as leaders, but there is no evidence that any such men were given attributes of divinity. The royal tombs, on the other hand, suggest a class of nobility whose human attributes were overshadowed by their presumed divine qualities.

WRITING

Early written documents were found at Ur, and these merit special discussion since writing had such a profound effect on the development of civilization. The history of writing is a fascinating and complex study in itself, and only a cursory summary can be given here. The beginning of civilization is conventionally recognized by the beginning of writing; in a sense, the advent of writing is also the beginning of history since it marks the first permanent records of human language and thought. Until there was writing, each generation had to learn from the preceding generation, and transmitted knowledge was limited by the fallibility of human memory. After writing began, knowledge could be stored and reproduced, to be consulted whenever required. The development of human knowledge was therefore vastly expanded as soon as a writing system was invented.

True writing, the use of symbols to represent ideas and events, is not simply a series of pictures. If ancient man drew a picture of two men and an elephant, the image of men and elephant would be communicated, but the meaning of the picture was known only to the maker. The message might be, variously, "Two men killed an elephant," "An elephant killed two men," or even, "Joe and I killed an elephant." But all that is communicated by the picture is the idea of men and elephants. True writing must communicate more explicitly by representing the words of speech.

Such true writing does occur at Ur, in several periods, starting with simple and limited written texts dating from the time of the royal tombs and slightly before, in the late Uruk period about 3500 B.C. (Writing was used in Egypt at about this time but with a different set of symbols.) The writing at Ur and other Sumerian cities consists of conventional signs inscribed on clay bricks. The earliest writing represents accounts (tallies of offerings and the like) and short inscriptions giving the names of rulers and deities. Shortly after the time of the royal tombs, writing blossoms into a vast body of business documents, including bills of sale, contracts, wills, and similar records. Many of the most interesting of the early writings have been published by Kramer (1959) in his book *History Begins at Sumer*. This book makes clear the greatly amplified picture of ancient life that can be obtained in regions where written documents survive. From written records, we have direct access to knowledge and thoughts of the ancient people, whereas inference from objects alone is only an indirect way of getting such information.

Even from this brief summary of the finds made at Ur, it is

Fig. 24. An example of early writing from approximately the time of the royal tombs at Ur. *A semipictographic stone tablet, about 5 inches square, from the site of Lagash and dating from about 2500 B.C. The tablet records a sale of land to Enhegal, king of Lagash. Photograph from S. N. Kramer and the University of Pennsylvania Museum.*

apparent that we are presented with a much more complex picture of human culture than we have seen in the sites previously discussed. Although it is difficult to reduce the large amount of information on such a rich and complex society to a short summary, the basic adaptations of the peoples in cities like Ur can be analyzed in much the same way that applies to simpler sites.

ADAPTATION TO ENVIRONMENT

The business of making a living at Ur was a matter of successful farming. Most of the population of Ur, probably well over 90 per cent, consisted of farming families. Some wild animals were obtained, like deer, and fishing seems to have been of some importance. The Ur people sowed grain (mostly barley and emmer wheat) in small plots irrigated by community canals. Daily routine included tending the fields and repairing the canals (a full-time job). Crops were harvested with a small hand sickle, and most of the work was done by human labor, although domestic animals were available: donkeys, cattle, sheep, goats, and pigs. A very simple plow was pulled by a donkey. This kind of peasant agriculture increased man's control over his environment to the extent that an economic surplus could be accumulated to support ruling classes, construct temples, and do many things not previously possible in human history. Today, five thousand years later, similar peasant agriculture, often utilizing the same crops and the same domestic animals, provides the basic economy of large areas of the world, and substantial improvement in the form of mechanized agriculture is only a little over a hundred years old.

Although agricultural knowledge was relatively simple at Ur, even in the period of the royal tombs some significant technological developments had taken place. Pottery making, important for vessels and containers, was common (Fig. 26). The people knew and used wheeled carts. They used tools of copper and bronze in addition to those of stone. Persons of noble rank had objects of gold and silver.

Engineering knowledge had also improved, and man was able to make his mark on nature in ways not previously possible. He constructed domes and vaults, irrigation systems, city walls, and massive temples, not to mention the cities themselves with their thousands of mud-brick homes. Although the people of Ur did not *control* nature (any more than we do), the ancient farmers *coped*

Fig. 25. Plaque from the Royal Cemetery at Ur. *About 6 inches wide. Animal figures, particularly cattle, play a prominent part in Sumerian art and religion. Specimen in the University of Pennsylvania Museum. Photograph by P. T. Furst.*

Fig. 26. Pottery vessel from the Royal Cemetery at Ur. *Although elaborate metal working was applied to some vessels (see Fig. 32, color), the commonplace pottery was the container for the common people and an occasional piece such as this one served as part of the offerings in the royal tombs. Specimen in the University of Pennsylvania Museum. Photograph by P. T. Furst. Diameter of vessel 9 inches.*

with nature in a basically modern way. Their attitude toward nature had changed from passive acceptance to deliberate attempts at managing plants, animals, and water supply. These attempts at control were by means of prayer or magical spell, as well as by planting, breeding, and engineering, but they represented a big step in the direction of modern developments.

ADAPTATION TO OTHER PEOPLE — POLITICAL AND SOCIAL ORGANIZATION

At the time of the royal cemetery, the surrounding area in Mesopotamia contained several other cities of size and importance comparable to Ur. It is safe to assume that these cities were similar in social and political organization, both during the period of the royal tombs and during dynasties immediately succeeding. Much can therefore be inferred about the Ur of the royal tombs from the documentary records of these slightly later dynasties. Each of the Sumerian cities, and probably those further north also, had a presiding deity with his temple and priests. At Ur, the patron deity seems to have been the moon god, his chief priest the governor of the city and its lands, serving as the vice-regent of the deity. In early times he was titled "the tenant farmer of the god" — that is, the land was believed to belong to the god and the worldly ruler is simply a "foreman" supervising the farming activities. Only when the priest-ruler's control extended to include other cities did he adopt a title comparable to *king*. Archaeological reconstruction of these details is based upon written records, preserved as archaeological specimens in the form of inscribed bricks and tablets of stone and clay.

Politically, therefore, there were series of city-states with now one, now another being dominant. Ur was the ruling city-state in the early dynastic period, but control soon passed to other communities and for most of its history Ur was subject to the rule of other cities. It always had its own priest-ruler, however, whether or not he was subject to outside political controls.

Within the city each individual had a definite place in the social system, his position being regulated by inheritance, wealth, and community service among other things. Several social classes were recognized — at the top, members of the royal class, equivalent almost to gods; at the bottom, slaves who were owned by others and did the menial labor. The slaves were most often war captives but could be bought and sold. Between royalty and slaves were several other ranks — merchants, warriors, artisans, and lesser nobility. Reconstruction of this social system is based on several kinds of archaeological finds. Most important is direct evidence from archaeological inscriptions and portrayal of social distinctions in the art, such as the symbols of rank commonly shown. Also valuable are the indications of wealth and power suggested by differences in housing, material possessions, and mortuary treatment for the several classes of people.

Specialization of labor was well developed by this time. In the earliest hunting and gathering societies, everyone lived much the same sort of life, accumulating food and attending to his own needs by manufacturing his own tools and weapons. But with the development of agriculture and fixed communities, technology developed to the point where full-time specialists were needed to produce many goods. The gold ornaments at Ur, for example, show too much skill to have been made by a person who did not devote his whole time and attention to this task. Undoubtedly most of the people at Ur were farmers, but their surplus supported the craftsmen and laborers who built the temples and created all the art objects. And in addition to craftsmen, organized city life now needed government officials, scribes, teachers, priests, and armies, all of them supported by the food surplus produced by the farmers.

Political control within the community was well formalized by this time. With the development of writing, it became possible to prepare formal agreements (contracts) between individuals, and much early writing has this function. By 2000 B.C., the law required that all business transactions, even down to the smallest, be in writing and properly signed by the principals and witnesses. As early as the time of the Royal Cemetery at Ur, written records were kept on clay tablets of house rentals, mortgages, loans, wages, marriages, and wills. Interestingly to us, the business obligations were computed in quantities of grain, domestic animals, labor service, or other values, since money as coin or currency had not been invented.

It is apparent that somebody in the community controlled and organized the labor necessary for constructing community projects such as irrigation ditches, city walls, and large temples. It can be assumed that rulers had considerable autocratic authority over their subjects, that the primitive democracy of hunting and gath-

Fig. 28. Limestone statuette from Khafaje, Iraq. *Height 9 inches. Dating from 2600 B.C., the time of the royal tombs at Ur, this figure in the University of Pennsylvania Museum is a good example of Sumerian sculpture in its representation of human figures. Photograph by P. T. Furst.*

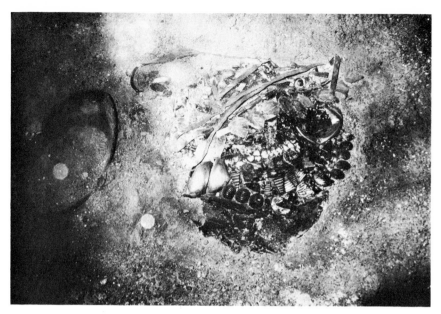

Figure 29. Jewelry from Ur. *A mass of jewels as found with two attendants in a royal tomb at Ur, displayed at the University of Pennsylvania Museum; the jewelry and the block of site material are displayed intact. The jewelry as shown covers an area about two feet in diameter. Photograph by P. T. Furst.*

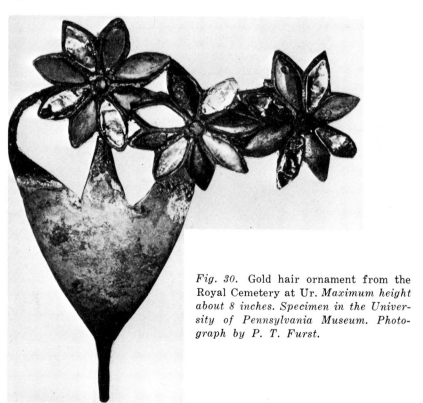

Fig. 30. Gold hair ornament from the Royal Cemetery at Ur. *Maximum height about 8 inches. Specimen in the University of Pennsylvania Museum. Photograph by P. T. Furst.*

93

ering societies, where each man is his own boss, was not a feature of Bronze Age cities such as Ur.

Although the world of Ur was still small and limited, the ancient city dwellers were well on the way to becoming cosmopolitan. Long-distance trading expeditions were necessary to get important materials (such as gold or copper), and although the average man probably spent his life without going far from home, some individuals traveled several hundred miles on trading trips. However, people of the earliest cities do not seem to have been too successful at organizing intercommunity efforts; each city maintained its independence even when alliance was imperative to defend against outside invaders. The cities fought against one another; stone monuments or *stelae,* commemorating the victory of one city over another, are useful documents. Each city-state maintained its own army.

SATISFACTION OF THE "INNER MAN" THROUGH RELIGION

By the time of ancient Ur, the importance of religion had greatly increased. Concern with the dead and provision for their afterlife appropriate to their position on earth was evident, and religion dominated many aspects of daily life. A priestly class served a formalized religion with many named deities, elaborate rituals, and great expenditure of labor on temples. The layman was, no doubt, more spectator than participant in much of this activity (except for the labor of construction), but he observed public religious ceremonies and knew his gods and the priests who served as intermediaries between gods and men.

Although vastly more complex than the religion of Paleolithic man, the religions in the agricultural cities were similar in that they were closely related to the business of making a living. The citizens of Ur shared the concept of the cave dwellers that a greater-than-human force was necessary to insure man's prosperity. Upper Paleolithic man sought to create his game animals through ritual art; the citizens of Ur called on deities to bring rain and cause the fields and herds to prosper. A famous frieze from Al-Ubaid (near Ur) shows a dairy scene with men milking cattle and straining the milk into large storage vessels. Because of the costume of the men and the great care in carving this work of art in limestone and shell, it is believed that it is not simply a farm scene, but a portrayal of religious activity. Man's control over his environment, as represented in plant and animal domestication, had important religious connotations.

Art and Learning

In Ur, because of writing, "higher learning" became possible, and members of the priestly class began seeking knowledge of such fields as mathematics and astronomy. Art and luxury goods were well established and the crafts of the artisan developed artistic representations of humans and animals, as well as aesthetic work in pottery, metal, and other materials. Even the common people had some objects of adornment and luxury, and all could enjoy the painted and decorated exteriors of community temples.

To sum up, the earliest of developed towns had many features familiar in the cities of today. Perhaps the major difference was rule by a priesthood, without the separation of church and state characteristic of most modern governments. Other features of city life were closer to modern conditions: dependence on agricultural produce grown by a farming class, civic government regulating many aspects of life, and a diversity of occupations and social groups.

Selected References

The final reports on Ur have appeared in the series: Publications of the Joint Expedition of the British Museum and of the Museum of the University of Pennsylvania to Mesopotamia. There are five volumes of ancient texts and several more dealing with the actual operations, including Hall and Woolley (1927) and Woolley (1934). Other works in the list below are more general.

Chiera, Edward
1938   *They Wrote on Clay.* University of Chicago Press, Chicago. A popular account of the invention of writing with illustrations of early documents and discussion of their decipherment. Also available in paperback edition, Phoenix Books, 1956.

Frankfort, Henri
1956   *The Birth of Civilization in the Near East.* Doubleday and Company, New York. As the title indicates, a volume dealing with origins of civilization in Egypt and Mesopotamia. Good additional reading on the cultural context of the examples given in this book; includes a useful appendix on early contacts between Mesopotamia and Egypt.

HALL, H. R., and C. LEONARD WOOLLEY
1927   *Ur Excavations*. Volume I, Al-Ubaid. Oxford University Press, New York, London. Publications of the Joint Expedition of the British Museum and of the Museum of the University of Pennsylvania to Mesopotamia. Published for the Trustees of the Two Museums.

KRAMER, SAMUEL N.
1959   *History Begins at Sumer*. Anchor Books, Doubleday and Co., New York. Translates and discusses a number of the first written documents, ancient Sumerian writings which represent the first written record of many cultural features, including the first legal, ethical and philosophical writing, as well as the first case of "apple polishing" and the first library catalog. Shows clearly the vast enrichment of the archaeological record in those areas where written documents can be found.

1963   *The Sumerians, Their History, Culture, and Character*. University of Chicago Press, Chicago. A more general history than the work above, again based directly on translations of Sumerian documents.

PIGGOTT, STUART, editor
1961   *The Dawn of Civilization*. McGraw-Hill Book Co., New York, London. A series of articles dealing with the beginnings of civilization in all parts of the world. Includes discussion of Ur and the Sumerians. With almost a thousand very good illustrations, this is one of the best books summarizing the origin and spread of civilization.

WOOLLEY, C. LEONARD
1934   *Ur Excavations, Volume II, The Royal Cemetery*. Text and plates separately bound. Publications of the Joint Expedition of the British Museum and of the Museum of the University of Pennsylvania to Mesopotamia. Published for the Trustees of the Two Museums by the Aid of a Grant from the Carnegie Corporation of New York.

1946   *Ur: The First Phases*. Penguin Books, London.

1954   *Excavations at Ur: a Record of Twelve Years' Work*. E. Benn, London. A later summary. Summary of the author's excavations at Ur, written for the general reader.

6 EGYPT:
The Tomb of Tutankhamen

On November 26, 1922, one of archaeology's most dramatic and spectacular discoveries was seen for the first time as the archaeologist Howard Carter drilled a small hole through a walled-up door to look into the tomb chamber of Tutankhamen, pharaoh of Egypt at the end of the eighteenth dynasty. Since that king was laid to rest, nearly 3300 years had gone by. The discovery of the almost intact pharaonic tomb of 1350 B.C. attracted world-wide attention. Because of the elaborate and valuable objects (many of gold), this find has been cited in most popular books on archaeology. For this book, the tomb of Tutankhamen serves as an example in the development of civilization. The wealth and variety of objects in the tomb give a good picture of Egyptian life at a particular time and permit a number of archaeological inferences. Not all the objects in the tomb were gold and ornamental; the many more mundane articles included bows and arrows, food (bread and wine), and such things as wooden chests containing the king's underwear. Many Egyptian manufactures, previously known only through pictures in tomb paintings, were found.

Tutankhamen's tomb is over a thousand years later than the royal tombs of Ur and it shows some general advances of human knowledge. But though Egypt and the Sumerian area had contacts from very early times, it must not be assumed that they followed identical paths of development. Egypt developed its own writing, art style, religion, and way of life, wherefore Egyptian civilization has a unique pattern of its own. On the other hand, all the cities of the ancient world shared in the increasing knowledge and complexity accrued from civilized life over many generations. The objects in Tutankhamen's tomb show some of these significant advances.

TABLE 4. CHRONOLOGICAL SUMMARY: EGYPT

Date	Period	Dynasty
Since A.D. 640	Arab	—
30 B.C. to A.D. 640	Roman	—
332-30	Greek (Ptolemaic)	—
525-332	Persian	27 to 30
1090-525	Late Egyptian Period	21 to 26
1572-1090	New Kingdom	18 to 20
2475-1572	Middle Kingdom	7 to 17
2980-2475	Old Kingdom	3 to 6
3200-2980	Protodynastic	1 and 2
3350-3200	Late Gerzean	Predynastic
3500-3350	Early Gerzean	Predynastic
3800-3500	Amratian	Predynastic
4100-3800	Badarian	Predynastic
Ca. 9,000 or 10,000 B.C. to 5,000 B.C.*	Neolithic	Late Stone Age

*No known Neolithic sites in Egypt are of the maximum age given; the beginning date is speculative.

TABLE 5. CHRONOLOGY OF THE EGYPTIAN EIGHTEENTH DYNASTY
(AFTER PIANKOFF, 1955)

Pharaoh	Reign
Horemheb	1346-1315
Ay	1349-1346
Tutankhamen	1357-1349
Semenkhare	1359-1357*
Akhenaton (Amenophis IV)	1373-1357*
Amenophis III	1402-1365*
Thutmosis IV	1417-1402
Amenophis II	1450-1417
Thutmosis III	1503-1450*
Hatshepsut	1503-1482
Thutmosis II	1512-1503
Thutmosis I	1528-1512
Amenophis I	1550-1528
Ahmose	1572-1550

*Overlapping of dates is due to coregencies.

A ROYAL CEMETERY

Tutankhamen's tomb was found in the Valley of the Kings, a rocky canyon situated in the hills across the Nile from modern Luxor (ancient Thebes). The canyon served as a royal cemetery starting with the eighteenth dynasty in Egypt. At this time, the practice of burial in pyramids was abandoned and royal tombs were constructed of chambers cut into solid rock. Here in the valley near Thebes, some 400 miles south of Cairo, about forty royal tombs were constructed. Of these, only two were still occupied by their royal tenants when found by archaeologists: the tomb of Amenophis II (found in 1898) and the tomb of Tutankhamen. All the rest had been plundered centuries in the past; as in all areas of the world where rich offerings are buried, the business of tomb robbings flourishes. The really remarkable thing about Tutankhamen's tomb was that it remained almost unaltered, since even this one had been entered at least twice by robbers in ancient times. Now, of all the kings formerly buried in the royal tombs of the Valley of the Kings, only Tutankhamen still rests in the tomb built for him. His mummy was returned to the tomb after study and he lies in the sarcophagus (see Fig. 33, color section) of the burial chamber. The sarcophagus lid, four gilded shrines, and the wealth of other objects found in the burial chamber have all been removed to the Cairo Museum.

The archaeologist Howard Carter had been working in the Valley of the Kings from 1917 to 1922 without success in finding new tombs. In his last scheduled season, his workers unearthed the remains of some simple huts that had housed the construction laborers who built one of the later tombs. Beneath the foundation of the huts, a staircase was found leading to a tunnel filled with rubble, at the end of which lay the multiroom tomb chamber. The tomb consisted of four rooms, all with mortuary offerings, and in one lay the king. The anteroom alone contained over 700 objects, including life-size wooden statues of the king, chests containing household goods, furniture, and vessels of bronze, alabaster, and glass. Many seasons of work were required to remove and restore all the specimens. The one tomb yielded literally a museumful of ancient Egyptian manufactures, many of which can be seen today in the Cairo Museum.

A tomb, by its very nature, yields more information on the religious and aesthetic adaptations of the ancient Egyptians than

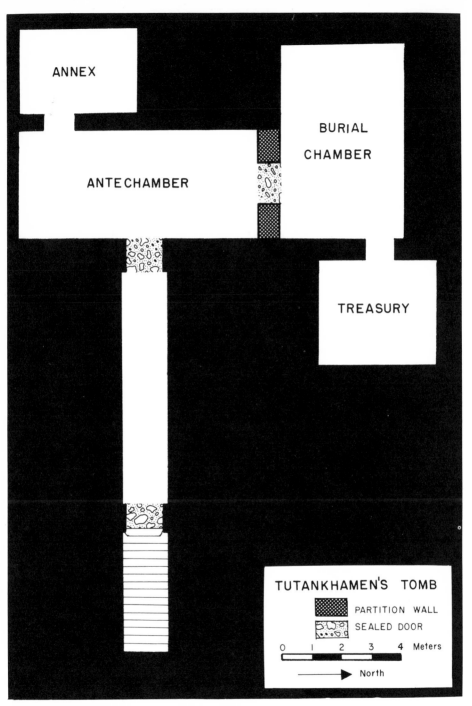

ANNEX

BURIAL
CHAMBER

ANTECHAMBER

TREASURY

TUTANKHAMEN'S TOMB

PARTITION WALL
SEALED DOOR

0   1   2   3   4   Meters

North

Fig. 34. Plan of Tutankhamen's tomb as cut into the rock of the Valley of the Kings. *Although small and simple in comparison with other tombs in the same valley, the wealth of objects which filled the four rooms of this tomb rank it as one of the major archaeological discoveries of all time. Redrawn after Carter and Mace (1923–1933).*

Fig. 35. The antechamber to Tutankhamen's tomb as it appeared when first entered by the archaeologists. *Against the left wall is a large bed in animal form and the room is full of chests of goods, furniture, weapons, and vessels. Between the two large wooden figures in the upper photo is a sealed doorway leading to the burial chamber. The oval wooden containers in the lower photo contained food for the departed king. Photograph by Harry Burton, The Metropolitan Museum of Art.*

on their more secular affairs such as making a living. However, the thousands of objects recovered from Tutankhamen's tomb included some that throw light on man's basic adaptations. The published accounts tend to stress the artistic objects from the tomb and to mention the utilitarian briefly, if at all. Yet in the tomb there is evidence, both direct and indirect, for almost every phase of contemporary human life.

THE EGYPTIAN ECONOMY

Amid the elaborate and costly objects buried with Tutankhamen was a humble but highly significant offering of several loaves of bread, still preserved in open-work basketry containers. Intended as food for the departed pharaoh, the bread symbolizes the agricultural basis for Egyptian civilization — the means of support without which neither the tomb nor all it stands for could have existed. The highly developed and intensive agriculture of Egypt supplied the wealth to maintain the social order and permit the elaboration of art and religion.

Modern schoolchildren hear of the river Nile and its importance to the development of ancient Egypt, for the Nile watered the crops and its annual flooding restored the soil by depositing a rich silt layer. Even modern Egypt is essentially a green cultivated strip divided by the Nile, surrounded by dry and sterile desert. The ancient Egyptians fully appreciated the importance of the Nile to their prosperity, and from the earliest dynasties a careful record was kept of the height reached by the Nile each year. A number of hymns to the Nile reflect the importance of the river to Egyptian thought: the complete dependence of the civilization on agriculture, and in turn on the Nile, which alone makes farming possible in Egypt. However, the hymns to the Nile are not mere secular accounts about life on the farm but are embodied in sacred writings and often refer to the god-king as well as to the Nile and the crops.

By the time of Tutankhamen, the advantages of agriculture over hunting and gathering were fully realized, and after several millenia of cultivation the peasant farmers had become able to support a dense population. Though drought and famine occurred and though the majority of the workers were occupied in tilling the soil, the Egyptian adaptation to environment was more efficient than that of earlier peoples.

The Nile was also the chief route of transportation for both goods and people. Tutankhamen's tomb contains models of sailing boats and paddles (of magical import, for transporting the soul to the other world) and a statuette of the king standing in a rush canoe.

EGYPTIAN TECHNOLOGY

Nearly every object in Tutankhamen's tomb shows the work of skilled artisan. A wide variety of materials was used, and the mastery shown by the Egyptians is in interesting contrast with the beginning efforts of man's history, when the planning and execution even of such a crude chopper as Peking man's seemed a great accomplishment.

One of the most important technological advances in human history is evidenced in Tutankhamen's tomb by several objects made of iron. How to smelt and work iron was discovered in Asia Minor before Tutankhamen's time, but in Egypt iron was a rare metal just beginning to come into use. Nearly all the metal in Tutankhamen's tomb is copper, bronze, gold, or silver. It is clear that iron was too rare and costly to be available to the common man and even royalty possessed little of it. The iron objects in the tomb include:

An iron-bladed dagger with gold handle and scabbard, believed imported from the north. It is not impossible that the dagger was a gift from a foreigner, perhaps a Hittite king.

A symbolic miniature head rest and an amuletic eye set in a gold bracelet. These were found with the mummy of the king, indicating the high value placed on iron.

A set of 16 chisels with full-size wooden handles but very small and thin iron parts, the total weight of all the metal being only about 4 grams. Apparently these tools were objects of ceremonial rather than functional importance.

The many examples of skilled workmanship found in the tomb, not only in metal but also in stone, pottery, wood, ivory, and other materials, show that many full-time specialized artisans were at work in Egyptian society. Here was a significant division of labor. However, the energy necessary to obtain and work the raw materials was still largely human energy. A tremendous expenditure of human labor went into the creation of individual articles, years

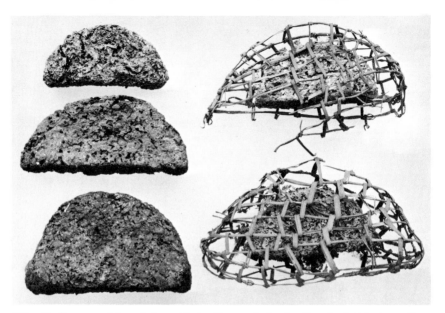

Fig. 36. Loaves of bread from Tutankhamen's tomb. *Bread of this type (two loaves are in openwork basketry containers) and form is still used in folk Egypt. The successful agriculture that permitted such bread to be a staple food supported ancient Egypt and provided the basis for civilization. Photograph by Harry Burton, The Metropolitan Museum of Art.*

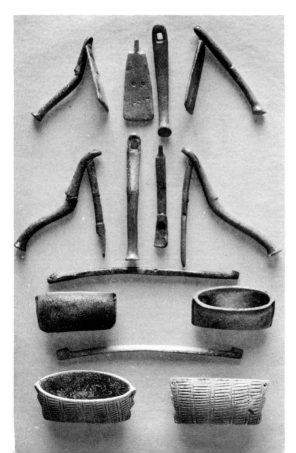

Fig. 37. Miniature agricultural implements (a couple of inches long) from Tutankhamen's tomb. *Extensive sets of such implements were found (here including picks, hoes, carrying yokes, and containers for harvested grain). In the tradition of providing the dead ruler with all the necessities of earthly life, these miniatures are symbolic of the farming that provided the subsistence base. Photograph by Harry Burton, The Metropolitan Museum of Art.*

Fig. 38. Pottery wine jars from Tutankhamen's tomb. *Photograph by Harry Burton, The Metropolitan Museum of Art.*

Fig. 39. Model boat (46 inches long) in place as it was found in Tutankhamen's tomb. *Several such boats were found in the tomb; they are believed to be representative of the funeral pilgrimage of the soul. As technological documents they provide abundant detail of ancient ship construction. Photograph by Harry Burton, The Metropolitan Museum of Art.*

Fig. 40. Model of a grinding stone from Tutankhamen's tomb. *An important tool in adaptation to the environment, representing the grinding of seeds to produce flour for bread — then as now the "staff of life" for peoples practicing grain agriculture. (Compare Figs. 69 and 80.) Photograph by Harry Burton, The Metropolitan Museum of Art.*

Fig. 41. Iron dagger from Tutankhamen's tomb. *This is one of the few iron objects found. It is about 9 inches long. Iron was just beginning to be known in Egypt at this time. Photograph by Harry Burton, The Metropolitan Museum of Art.*

Fig. 42. Set of chisels with wooden handles from Tutankhamen's tomb. *The small amount of iron used (only 4 grams total; the longest chisel is 15.5 centimeters over-all) suggests that these tools had a ritual meaning rather than a functional purpose. Photograph by Harry Burton, the Metropolitan Museum of Art.*

for some of the more elaborate items such as the gilded shrines over the king's body.

EGYPTIAN SOCIETY

In considering how the Egyptians of Tutankhamen's time organized their relationships to other people, the most immediate and striking feature is "big government." The area and population of ancient Egypt required complicated administrative machinery, and few features of modern government organization were unknown to the ancient Egyptians. By the time of Tutankhamen, the Egyptians had had 1,500 years of developing their bureaucracy and administration — wars and treaties, armies and navies, tax collectors and government bureaucrats, were all familiar to the Egyptian of the eighteenth dynasty.

Similar to the political organization of ancient Ur, Egyptian government was headed and validated by the pharaoh, who in his role as a living god added religious authority to civil actions. However, Egypt was no city state maintaining a tenuous control over a few square miles of territory, but a nation facing problems of internal unity and problems of international affairs with other countries, some hostile, some friendly, and some important for trade and raw materials. To the north, across the eastern tip of the Mediterranean, lay the kingdom of the Hittites, sufficiently powerful and important that royal marriages sometimes took place between the reigning houses of the Egyptians and the Hittites. To the northeast, Syria and Palestine were powers to be reckoned with. To the south, important trade connections existed with Ethiopia, Nubia, and various areas of Negro Africa. The political organization of ancient Egypt was far greater, in both size and complexity, than anything of this kind at Ur.

The complexity of Egyptian government at the time of Tutankhamen is well illustrated by the Egyptian army. During the eighteenth dynasty, threatened by outside invaders, Egypt developed a large standing army, which drew its recruits from all over the country and was officered by professional soldiers of several ranks. At least during the middle of the eighteenth dynasty, Egypt was a first-class military power, probably as great as any that had existed in the world up to that time. The Egyptian army was organized into divisions of about 5,000 men each; as many as four of these divisions could be mustered by the pharaoh. Each divi-

Fig. 43. Arrows and bows from Tutankhamen's tomb. *These show a variety of points used for warfare and hunting. Although these weapons of royalty are relatively elaborate in decoration, they exemplify the prevailing "bow and arrow" technology of ancient civilizations. Photographs by Harry Burton, The Metropolitan Museum of Art.*

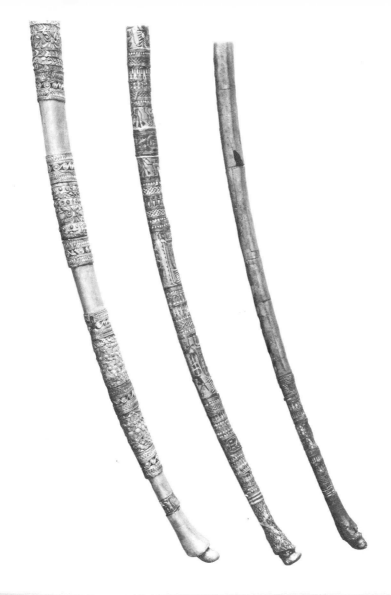

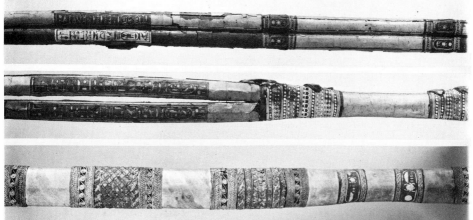

sion included both infantry and chariotry; cavalry had not yet been developed. The chariotry consisted of two-wheel two-horse chariots, each with a driver and a fighting soldier who carried bow and arrows, spear and shield. The infantry was divided into groups of soldiers, some archers, some armed with clubs and axes, some armed with shields and spears. (Figs. 43 and 44 show weapons from the tomb). Like modern armies, the Egyptian army was divided into groups of decreasing size, the smallest unit of which corresponded to a modern squad of ten or eleven men and was apparently headed by a common soldier. The lowest ranking officer commanded a group of about fifty men, the next higher in rank a company of about 250. The divisions of 5,000 men were commanded, at least in some cases, by royal princes. At the head of the whole army was the pharaoh, who often took personal leadership in major campaigns. The tomb of Tutankhamen shows many representations of the young pharaoh leading his troops in battle from a royal chariot, and the tomb contained such a chariot with its royal trappings, along with military accoutrements. Much of this art may be symbolic of the pharaoh's leadership rather than historical account of his campaigns, although the youthful Tutankhamen apparently participated in some military activities.

Although the Egyptian army was small by modern standards, it was a military organization in every sense, and the fact that the pharaoh could send several thousand soldiers on an expedition to a distant land demonstrates the economic and political development of the time. To field such an army required surplus wealth in order to feed and pay the troops, to maintain a quartermaster corps and transportation and supply systems, and to support the whole class of artisans needed to make the chariots, weapons, and other military gear required. The army is evidence of a wealthy, complex, and well-organized bureaucracy.

An insight into the politics of ancient Egypt can be had in the representations of slaves and captives found in Tutankhamen's tomb. Among the most interesting of these is a staff which indicates a bound Negro captive and similarly bound Asian captive. The king's footstool also portrays bound captives. Such finds, like the representations of Tutankhamen leading the troops and destroying his enemies, may be partly symbolic of the pharaoh's dominance, but they also reflect the real political situation during

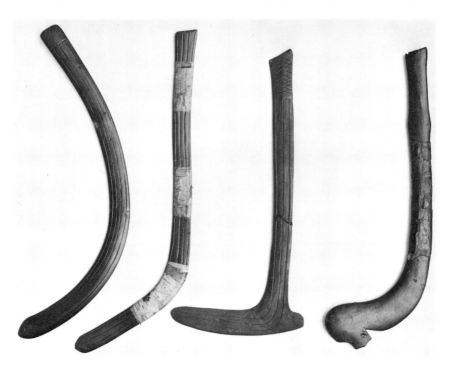

Fig. 44. Throwing clubs from Tutankhamen's tomb. *Part of a wide variety of weapons (for warfare and hunting) found in the tomb. Photograph by Harry Burton, the Metropolitan Museum of Art.*

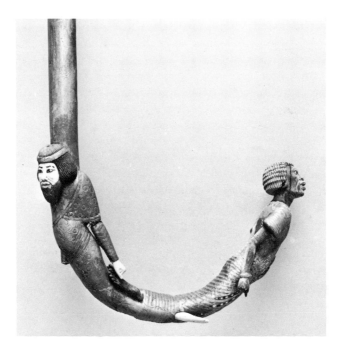

Fig. 45. Detail of a famous staff from Tutankhamen's tomb. *The figures show as bound captives a Negro and an Asian, and represent the military dominance of Egypt over surrounding peoples. Photograph by Harry Burton, The Metropolitan Museum of Art.*

much of the eighteenth dynasty. The Egyptians fought other Near Eastern peoples and maintained a chain of border forts in the south through which they received ivory and Negro slaves.

The military structure exemplifies a complex social order, but does not necessarily indicate a society dominated by military affairs. Other aspects of Egyptian life were equally complex, including the class organization of the priests, government servants, and artisans. The common man's life was affected by the welfare of the nation in a way not too different from that of his modern counterpart. The common man paid taxes and served in the army, grew the crops and built the monuments. When the nation prospered, he prospered; and when the nation suffered militarily or economically, the effects extended down to his ordinary life. The welfare of the individual was bound up with the welfare of the larger group, and he was vitally affected by events in foreign countries.

The elaboration of Tutankhamen's tomb testifies to a social position greatly exalted over that of other people. Both in the wealth of his physical possessions and in the many symbols of rank traditional in Egyptian society the king was marked off as the supreme member of the nobility. The pharaoh is depicted holding a crook and a flail, comparable to the mace as a badge of office. He wears a royal headdress, like a crown, and objects intended for his use often bear the royal name, marked off from other writing by enclosure in an oval symbol called a cartouche. Such clear-cut and constantly reiterated recognition of social rank implies a rather rigid social order with little opportunity for the individual to leave the class he was born in. Certainly inherited rank played a great part in Egyptian society. Yet the social classes were not rigid castes; there was apparently a certain amount of what the sociologists call social mobility, in which individuals could change their social rank through ability and industry. Individuals in one profession might move to another. Many personal success stories are recorded in the inscriptions. The story of Moses, adopted and raised as an Egyptian prince, indicates that a non-Egyptian could become important. Negroes attained high rank and even entered the royal family. Generals became pharaohs, and many men advanced markedly in positions of public trust. This tendency of the ancient Egyptians to seek and utilize talent when it appeared may

Fig. 47. Symbols of supremacy. *Royal headdress, crook, and flail. The upper part of the third (innermost) coffin of Tutankhamen, of richly decorated gold. (Compare Fig. 33.) Photograph by Harry Burton, The Metropolitan Museum of Art.*

have contributed to the persistence and dynamism of ancient Egyptian culture.

EGYPTIAN RELIGION

Although all cultures since Neanderthal man have had a concern with death and the afterlife, the ancient Egyptians carried this concern to such lengths that the most important event for an ancient Egyptian was his funeral. Although many historical factors led to this development, two features of Egyptian religion have particular significance. First was the belief that it was important for the mortal remains to be preserved, wherefore the practice of mummification to preserve the body and the construction of massive tombs designed to prevent damage. Second was the common primitive belief that objects placed with the dead could be used by the spirit in afterlife. Hence the wealth of objects placed in the tomb: food, water and wine, cosmetics, tools, weapons, and material objects used by the living. If the real objects were lacking, magical representations of them were substituted in the form of paintings on the tomb walls, or miniature models made of wood or clay.

The attention to funeral ritual was closely linked to the wealth and importance of the deceased. For the common man, a grave in the sand with a few pottery vessels was sufficient. An important person had a tomb cut into the rock of a mountain, and for the pharaoh the resources of the entire country could be called into the funeral preparation. Probably no mortals have ever been laid to rest with greater pomp and circumstance than Egyptian kings. Even such a relatively insignificant monarch as Tutankhamen was buried in a tomb of magnificent conception and execution.

Neglecting aesthetic elements, consider the physical steps necessary in the burial of Tutankhamen. The king's mummy, after elaborate mortuary procedures, was wrapped in a cloth embellished with many gold objects. Within the wrappings, next to the king's body, lay 143 separate items, mostly jewelry and amulets. The mummy was placed in a solid gold coffin, shaped to fit the king's body. The coffin in turn was laid inside another coffin, and still another, making three nested coffins in all. These were placed in a sculptured sarcophagus, a block of yellow quartzite nine feet long. The sarcophagus lid, a separate piece, weighed 2,500 pounds.

One would think that with three nested coffins and a massive stone sarcophagus the body of the king would be duly taken care of. But the sarcophagus was placed inside a wooden shrine, elaborately decorated on the exterior with gold work. Then three more such shrines were constructed over the innermost one, making a total of four. The outermost shrine is about ten by fifteen feet, the size of a small room. To protect the shrines and coffins, all were placed in a separate room of the tomb, itself a four-room structure with several sealed doors, cut more than fifty feet into the rock of the mountainside.

Before the archaeologists could see the person of Tutankhamen, therefore, they had to penetrate three sealed doors and four shrines, remove the sarcophagus lid with block and tackle, open three coffins, and finally unwrap the bindings of the mummy. When one thinks of the tremendous expenditure of labor and goods necessary for a royal funeral, it is easy to understand why the preparations had to go on all during the lifetime of the individual.

The people of ancient Ur provided a royal tomb not only with the material goods necessary to the dead ruler but also with sacrificed human retainers, including soldiers, musicians, and palace servants. These individuals were apparently put to death and placed in the tomb with the idea that their souls would join the soul of the dead king to serve him in the afterlife. The Egyptians also believed that the soul of a dead monarch should be provided with servants and retainers, but they made this provision in a symbolic rather than a literal way. They believed the representations of the tomb paintings could be magically used by the soul of the king. From early times the tombs contain small models and figures of servants which by magic were to become actual servants in the afterlife.

By the time of the eighteenth dynasty and the burial of Tutankhamen, an even greater degree of symbolism had developed and tombs were often provided with model tools such as hoes, picks, and buckets. Small figures also occur, the so-called *ushebti* figures. Most of these are mummiform and bear the name of the deceased as well as inscriptions from the Book of the Dead. It would be unseemly for royalty to do agricultural or other manual labor, and the ushebti figures show by their inscriptions that they were "volunteers" who were to step forward and perform whatever menial tasks might be demanded.

Egyptian culture is thus strongly colored by concern with im-

Fig. 48. Fire-making drill and hearth from Tutankhamen's tomb. *The highly civilized Egyptians used one of the oldest and simplest of fire-making devices. Photograph by Harry Burton, Metropolitan Museum of Art.*

Fig. 49. Baskets from Tutankhamen's tomb. *Typical of the many items of everyday life deposited in the tomb, baskets like these in form and technique are still widely made in folk Egypt. Photograph by Harry Burton, The Metropolitan Museum of Art.*

116

Fig. 50. Writing implements from Tutankhamen's tomb. *Writing had been known and used for over a thousand years by the time of Tutankhamen, so that archaeological interpretation can include direct historical evidence from the inscriptions. Photograph by Harry Burton, The Metropolitan Museum of Art.*

mortality and man's place in the universe. Although not everything in Egyptian life was devoted to thoughts of the afterlife, a great deal of it was. Much of the inscription and painting deals with religious and philosophical matters. The major works of art had a religious and magical significance, and, as is clearly shown by the tomb of Tutankhamen, the greatest creations of the craftsman, the artisan, and the artist were buried in tombs. The priests and philosophers of Egypt were much concerned with explaining the relationships between mortal humans and immortal gods and spirits. The elaborate paintings of four of the major eighteenth-dynasty tombs are in fact a theological composition: "The Book of What is in the Nether World." Although this writing is full of symbolism, it can be viewed as a guidebook, explaining to curious mortals the nature of the beings and happenings in the immortal world.

By the time of Tutankhamen's dynasty, Egyptian religion had been following the same basic pattern for over two thousand years. As a result, it had become complex and diverse, with many gods and ceremonies and with elaborate development of symbolism and ritual. To understand the theology of ancient Egypt requires at least as much study as to understand Christian theology, but the common man of Egypt may have had as little theological sophistication as the man in the street today. Then, as now, the religion of the common man must have consisted of the observance of religious customs without deep intellectual or philosophical understanding.

LIVING AND THE ARTS

Though the emphasis placed on mortuary practices suggests that an ancient Egyptian sought self-realization through "preparation for immortality," one should not visualize the Egyptians as brooding over impending death, nor as a people unable to realize fulfillment in the pleasures of the living world. The paintings and records show abundant scenes of banquets, concerts, and hunting and fishing expeditions (more important for sport than food) ; there is even one painting showing a man being carried home from a wine party. (Gaming boards with dice and markers were found in the tomb). To what extent these activities were available to the common man is uncertain, although it may be inferred that even the field workers had an occasional participation in festivals and the like.

Fig. 51. Gaming board with ivory playing pieces from Tutankhamen's tomb. *Games of this kind indicate much leisure; they are not found among the remains of peoples whose time had to be spent primarily in getting food. (Compare Fig. 83.) Photograph by Harry Burton, The Metropolitan Museum of Art.*

Fig. 52. Elaborate alabaster perfume vase from Tutankhamen's tomb. *Such finds reveal not only the skills of the artist and craftsman, but also show the wealth and social importance of the owner. Photograph by Harry Burton, The Metropolitan Museum of Art.*

Such creative activities as writing and art seem to have been the province of special classes, and again it seems unlikely that the common people participated very much for lack of time and training. However, finds from even the simple graves often show artistic embellishments, indicating that the general Egyptian population had a chance to enjoy and appreciate creativity in their lives.

EGYPT AND UR

To summarize briefly the finds from Tutankhamen's tomb that contrast with the royal tombs at Ur, more than a millenium older, new cultural elements include:

1. *Iron.* Tutankhamen's tomb is at the threshold of the Iron Age and hence shows more advanced technology than the royal tombs at Ur.
2. *More complex social structure.* The tomb representations of military activities and social rank attest a much larger political body and correspondingly greater social structure to deal with it.
3. *Greater sophistication in art and religion.* Both in the creation of art objects and in the much greater use of symbolism, Tutankhamen's tomb shows a richer expression of art and religion than the finds at Ur's royal tombs.
4. *Writing.* Although writing was beginning at the time of the royal tombs of Ur, by the time of Tutankhamen there existed a great body of literature and a much greater involvement of human life with written records. Much of the embellishment of objects in Tutankhamen's tomb consists of written inscriptions and even lengthy religious passages such as those on the shrines. Comparatively, the royal tombs at Ur show no such emphasis on use of writing.

SELECTED REFERENCES

CARTER, HOWARD, AND A. C. MACE
  1923-1933   *The Tomb of Tut-Ankh-Amen.* (3 vols.) George H. Doran Co., New York. Reprinted 1963 by Stechert-Hafner, New York. The original report by the discoverer of Tutankhamen's tomb. It contains 262 photographs of the tomb and its contents.

DESROCHES-NOBLECOURT, CHRISTIANE

1963   *Tutankhamen.* New York Graphic Society, New York. The best single-volume discussion of Tutankhamen's tomb, accompanied by 75 superb color photographs.

FAULKNER, R. O.

1953   Egyptian Military Organization. *Journal of Egyptian Archaeology,* Vol. 39, pp. 32-47. London. The military organization of ancient Egypt was used in this book to exemplify the complex social organization characteristic of Egyptian civilization. The data used in the present book are derived from Faulkner's scholarly and detailed article.

FOX, PENELOPE

1951   *Tutankhamun's Treasure.* Oxford University Press, London. Explanatory text and 72 excellently-reproduced plates showing Tutankhamen's tomb and objects found in it. Some of the plates are also printed in the report of Carter and Mace, others are not published elsewhere. The plates give a good selection of the more elaborate pieces from the tomb.

PIANKOFF, ALEXANDRE

1955   *The Shrines of Tut-Ankh-Amon.* Bollingen Series, Vol. 40, No. 2. Pantheon Books, New York.

1956   The Theology of the New Kingdom in Ancient Egypt. *Antiquity and Survival,* Vol. 1, pp. 488-500. The Hague.

The first mentioned is a detailed scholarly treatment of the inscriptions and decorations on the wooden shrine housing Tutankhamen's sarcophagus. The shrines bear religious symbols and theological writings. The second article is a more general discussion of theology based on the religious texts painted in tombs.

SHORTER, ALAN W.

1932   *An Introduction to Egyptian Religion. An Account of Religion in Egypt during the Eighteenth Dynasty.* Macmillan, New York.

WILSON, JOHN A.

1956   *The Culture of Ancient Egypt.* University of Chicago Press, Chicago. First published in clothbound edition under the title *The Burden of Egypt,* the Phoenix Books paperback includes the same text. An excellent one-volume summary of Egyptian history with interpretations and analyses as well as historical data.

7 FRINGES OF CIVILIZATION:
Sutton Hoo and Drakes Bay

THE SHIP BURIAL AT SUTTON HOO

So far our examples have proceeded along the path of ever-increasing complexity and wealth for the cultures mentioned. Starting with the earliest finds when man was first developing his attributes of humanity, and starting thus at the very beginning of man's knowledge of tool making, we find man's inventiveness and adaptability building in due course the striking ancient civilizations of the Old World. We now turn from such a comfortable, expectable, and seemingly inevitable path of progress to consider examples of peoples who did not share in the even advance of civilization. An excellent example is the royal burial place at Sutton Hoo, England. Evidence of a culture advanced in some ways, yet in some ways primitive compared to ancient Egypt, this archaeological discovery provides an excellent example to show that the path of change is not at all regular or even, let alone inevitable. It is a common assumption that an advantageous idea, once developed, will spread everywhere in a short time. However, the many peoples of the modern world who still have a very simple technology demonstrate the fallacy of the assumption, and in ancient times, when contact and communication between peoples were very limited, the spread or diffusion of new ideas and inventions was often very slow indeed.

While the complex civilizations of Egypt and the Near East were developing, most of the rest of the world remained at a much simpler cultural level for a long time after cities, writing, metalworking, and other complex features had appeared. An archaeological find providing a good example of this unequal cultural

TABLE 6. CHRONOLOGY OF BRITAIN

Date	Event and Culture
655 A.D.	Sutton Hoo ship burial
400 A.D.	Anglo-Saxons and their successors; modern history
43 A.D.	Romans
500 B.C.	Iron Age
1750 B.C.	Bronze Age
1900 B.C.	Beaker Invasions
2500 B.C.	Neolithic

growth is the burial place of an East Anglian king at Sutton Hoo dating from 655 A.D., two thousand years after Tutankhamen's time, and several hundred years after Roman civilization had come to England. The tomb at Sutton Hoo is the burial place of a king who would have been considered a barbarian by Roman or Near Eastern standards. The England of the period had a culture on the fringes of civilization — in contact with the higher civilizations and influenced by them, but maintaining many older practices in material culture, social organization, and religion.

Such a culture is referred to as *marginal*, a term which can have two meanings. It can be marginal: (1) in the cultural sense of representing survivals of older and simpler cultural features, or (2) in a geographic sense — far distant from the centers of civilization. Usually, both meanings apply together — the marginal cultures will usually be at a distance from the centers of advanced development and more simple culturally. There are some exceptions, but all the marginal cultures we consider here can be seen to exemplify both senses of the word. Often a marginal culture represents the apex of achievement in the particular region where it is found — it is marginal only by comparison to developments somewhere else.

Sutton Hoo is six miles from the coast at Woodbridge, about 100 miles northeast of London. This site originally had eleven artificial mounds ("barrows" in English usage), the biggest of which was 10 or 12 feet in height and about 150 feet in diameter. Some of these were investigated in 1938 and 1939 and found to contain burials and be intended as mortuary monuments. At least some of the mounds contained the remains of boats.

In April of 1939, excavations were made in the largest mound by Basil Brown, an amateur archaeologist affiliated with the Ipswich Museum. Preliminary digging at one end of the mound disclosed rusted iron nails arranged in a pattern where they had formerly fastened wooden planking; Brown correctly recognized that the mound had been built over a boat of considerable size. By May, much of the boat was exposed and government archaeologists and representatives of the British Museum were called in to carry on with a difficult and extremely important excavation. It soon became apparent that the ship belonged to the Anglo-Saxon age. In a burial chamber amidships were found gold jewelry, silver plate, weapons and bowls, the remains of cauldrons, buckets, and many other objects. No skeleton was found, and it seems that this ship burial was a cenotaph — an empty tomb built as a monument to a person whose remains are buried elsewhere or are lost.

One of the most difficult and suspenseful tasks for the archaeologist was the exposure and recording of the large buried boat (Figs. 54, 55). The moist sand did not preserve wood and other perishable objects except in the form of a discoloration or stain. The wooden planks of the boat were gone; even the iron nails of the ship were badly rusted and although in their proper relative positions lay loose in the sand. The excavation had to be done from the inside, working out until the stained layer was reached. This was exposed carefully, leaving the rusted nails in position, and from this painstaking task it was possible to reconstruct the whole boat with considerable accuracy and detail. Such a find in the ground can be easily obliterated by hasty or unthinking excavation; it is therefore a credit to the discoverer and the later excavators that such complete knowledge of the vanished boat was obtained. The patience of the archaeologists was rewarded by seeing more and more detail of the construction as the excavation proceeded, until at the conclusion of the work the entire boat lay revealed.

The boat was a large open rowing boat built to be propelled by 38 oarsmen. It measured some 80 feet in length, with a beam of 14

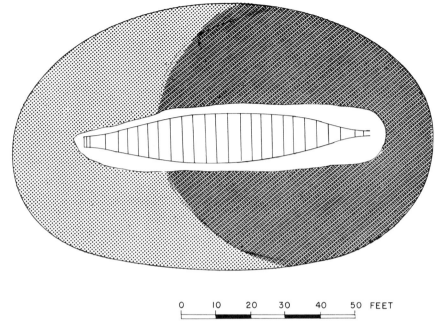

0   10   20   30   40   50 FEET

Fig. 54. Plan of the Sutton Hoo ship as exposed in the ground. *Shaded area indicates the extent of the mound over the ship; the lightly shaded portion is conjectural, that part of the mound having been leveled by agricultural activity through the years. Redrawn from Bruce-Mitford (1947).*

Fig. 55. The Sutton Hoo ship as finally exposed. *The impression of the stern section in the sand, exposing the impressions of wooden timbers and leaving the original iron rivets in position.* © *British Museum.*

feet and a prow rising at least 12½ feet above water. This ship, an old one showing previous use, had been hauled half a mile from the nearest estuary and lowered into a great pit dug in the sand. A specially built mortuary cabin amidships was then filled with offerings, the whole ship filled with sand, and the mound built above from the surrounding turf.

The central chamber containing the offerings revealed a wealth of early Anglo-Saxon art and skill. The items can be divided into two main groups: military trappings and symbols of rank (Figs. 56-59), and objects of wealth including a purse with 37 gold coins and a set of ten nested silver bowls (Figs. 60-62). One must conclude that the offerings were made in honor of a most important person; the cenotaph is the richest find of its period, and authorities are agreed that none but a royal personage could have received such a funeral.

The identity of the person for whom this complex mortuary offering was made, and the situation leading to his death, are subjects of great interest. Here the archaeologist must give way to the historian, for in the ordinary course of events archaeology is unable to provide names, historical details of specific occasions, or personal information. In the absence of written documents, archaeology is for the most part an impersonal study concentrating on the development of culture rather than on the important individuals and events of the past. Only occasionally does the archaeologist get a glimpse of some individual event or person; mostly he sees the results of human activity but not the motivations and actions of the individual actors in the human drama.

Sutton Hoo, however, is well within the period of written history and the find can be analyzed by the methods of the historian as well as by the methods of the archaeologist. Archaeology, in recovering the ship and its accompanying offerings, provides many physical evidences of art and technology which are poorly described in the historical documents and hence little known in detail. History, through analysis of contemporary documents, can provide details on the religion connected with the ship burial and can attempt identification of the circumstances and personages involved. From the historical records of the time, it is believed that the cenotaph is that of the East Anglian King Aethelhere, who is known to have been killed in the battle of Winwaed (Yorkshire) in 655 A.D.

Fig. 56. Iron and bronze helmet from Sutton Hoo. *Part of the military trap-pings of the ship burial and one of the indicators that the mortuary monument was in honor of a warrior king.* © *British Museum.*

Fig. 57. The great shield (restored) from Sutton Hoo. *The leather or wood of the original shield having disappeared in the ground, the reconstruction is based upon the relative positions of the metal ornaments and the central boss as they were discovered. The shield is 33 inches in diameter.* © *British Museum.*

Fig. 58. Sword and scabbard (partially restored). *This heavy sword some three feet long accompanied the shield, helmet, and other military trappings of the Sutton Hoo buried ship.* © *British Museum.*

128

Fig. 59. The scepter or "whetstone" from Sutton Hoo. *This stone object, decorated with human heads at both ends, is in the form of a whetstone but is interpreted as a scepter or symbol of authority, strengthening the belief that the mortuary deposit was for a royal personage.* © *British Museum.*

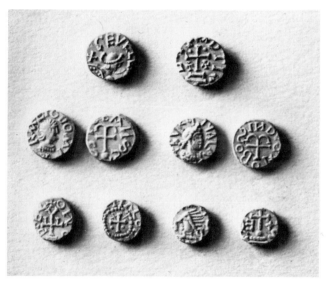

Fig. 60. Gold coins from Sutton Hoo. *Part of a group of 37 gold coins recovered from the central chamber of the Sutton Hoo ship. All were struck by the Merovingian kings of France and they date the ship burial as not prior to A.D. 650.* © *British Museum.*

Fig. 61. Decorated silver bowl from Sutton Hoo *(9 inches in diameter). One of several silver bowls recovered from Sutton Hoo. Aside from the indication these provide of the wealth and importance of the ship burial, they are notable in being derived from the Eastern Mediterranean region. Hence they indicate extensive culture contacts.* © *British Museum.*

Fig. 62. Hinged clasps from Sutton Hoo. *Made of gold, these ornaments were found near the sword and its fittings. They are between 4 and 5 inches long.* © *British Museum.*

Finds such as the buried Sutton Hoo ship have a double value, contributing as they do to both history and archaeology. The historian sees in this find the actual objects used by royalty in early English history — material confirmation and amplification of historical statements and allusions. The archaeologist rightly considers Sutton Hoo among the richest of treasures ever found in England; the specimens, many of which are on display at the British Museum, include spectacular examples of the ancient craftsman's art and skill.

Sutton Hoo also has another significance if it is examined from the viewpoint of comparative culture history. Since this find is a specialized mortuary construction for royalty, it can be compared with Tutankhamen's tomb, which served a similar purpose. Both entailed the expenditure of great community effort, although the Sutton Hoo burial required only a fraction of the construction time expended on Tutankhamen's tomb 2,000 years before. The two constructions also show the burial of wealth items of the two cultures to honor the departed ruler. A much more elaborate conception of the offering is seen in the tomb of Tutankhamen, where effort was made to include a complete sample of earthly products. To be sure, preservation must be considered in the comparison; many objects of wood or other perishable materials may have disintegrated at Sutton Hoo while their likes remain intact in Egypt's dry climate. Nonetheless, the Sutton Hoo ship burial is a simpler conception, a smaller effort and smaller accomplishment than the splendid mortuary complex of ancient Egypt.

Archaeological comparisons of such finds are not quite so simple and obvious as they first appear. Certainly the kings of ancient Egypt controlled more resources than those of early England. Certainly the apex achievements of the Egyptians overshadow those at Sutton Hoo. Yet these facts do not mean a general simplicity and inferiority for the English culture. Was the peasant farmer of Sutton Hoo worse off than the peasant farmer of ancient Egypt? We do not know, but we can guess that the lives of the common people were not too dissimilar and that in a few material ways (possession of metal tools, for example) the peasants of early England were better off than those of ancient Egypt.

In addition, even though the general mortuary complex of King Tutankhamen's tomb is vastly more impressive than the ship burial of Sutton Hoo, the archaeologist can see in the latter many features showing great culture advances over the knowledge of ancient Egypt. Specimens from Sutton Hoo that testify to advance over Egyptian knowledge include:

1. *Iron objects in quantity*. Whereas Tutankhamen's tomb had only a few small iron objects appearing as rare and precious items, the Sutton Hoo burial shows iron as a common utilitarian material. The ship was held together with iron nails; iron cauldrons, chains, and other iron objects were abundant in the tomb.
2. *Money*. Although wealth objects abound in Tutankhamen's tomb, nothing in the tomb can be classified as money — as a standardized medium of exchange. The purse of coins found at Sutton Hoo shows that the people of this site knew and used money — an important invention for economic relationships and greatly superior to the older system of barter.
3. *Alphabetic writing*. Ancient Egyptians had writing, but used hundreds of symbols since their writing expressed syllables rather than individual sounds. At Sutton Hoo, inscriptions in Greek letters show that alphabetic writing was known in the English culture of the time and that this region was more advanced in knowledge of effective writing techniques than ancient Egypt (Fig. 63). Though Britain had alphabetic writing from the time of the Romans, several hundred years prior to the Sutton Hoo burial, the archaeological evidence for writing in Anglo-Saxon England is not as abundant as one might expect, and the very limited inscriptions in the Sutton Hoo burial are the only direct archaeological indications of writing at this site (books and parchment would have disintegrated if placed in the tomb).

Although Sutton Hoo was marginal in its over-all wealth and complexity, and was simpler than contemporary and earlier sites some distance away, the people of Sutton Hoo shared in significant areas of knowledge with the advanced civilizations of the time. In the ways already mentioned they were superior to the ancient Egyptians. Thus a marginal culture is not one that stands still and learns nothing so that it preserves intact the pattern of a previous era. What is significant is that the marginal culture tends to get its culture advances slowly and by borrowing or copying the ideas from others. The examples mentioned (iron,

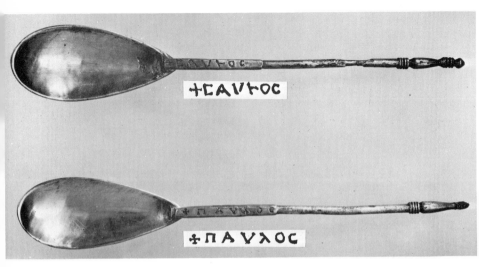

Fig. 63. Two silver spoons from the Sutton Hoo ship burial. *These two spoons are important because of their inscriptions "Saul" and "Paul" in Greek letters. Almost the only archaeological (as opposed to historical documentation) evidences that literacy and Christianity may have been known to the people who made the ship burial.* © *British Museum.*

money, and alphabetic writing) were all developed in the regions of Greece and Asia Minor centuries before the time of the people of Sutton Hoo; none of them show any creativity from within the Sutton Hoo population. Although the people of Sutton Hoo showed their own creativity in many of their manufactures, they were in the position of recipients of major ideas from outside rather than the innovators of such ideas.

Perhaps because of disintegration of any food offerings that may have been present, there is no direct archaeological evidence at Sutton Hoo of the environmental adaptation necessary to support the wealth revealed. There were no indications of food resources (except food vessels) in the ship, and one must pass over the question of food resources without tangible archaeological evidence. From historical records, it is clear that the people had attained the peasant farmer level, and one could infer as much from the technological skill revealed in the several items of Anglo-Saxon jewelry. The latter clearly were made by skilled specialists, a class whose presence indicates a food surplus to support the full-time artisan.

That the people of Sutton Hoo had contacts with the centers of civilization is shown by trade objects in the ship burial. The gold coins had come from France, and silver objects (including two spoons bearing the names "Saul" and "Paul" in Greek letters) had come from the central and eastern Mediterranean area. At least through trade the people of the ship burial were subject to influences from hundreds of miles away. The whole burial is also an indication of rank and social status, of the pomp and circumstance of royalty. Yet magnificent as the finds at Sutton Hoo are, artistically and intrinsically, they appear limited indeed in comparison with a royal tomb of Egypt, or even with those of still more ancient Ur. Many of the apex achievements of early England had been reached and surpassed by other civilizations thousands of years earlier.

To account for *why* one area attains greater complexity in shorter time, it is tempting (but superficial) to attribute the difference to environmental factors such as the availability of good land for agriculture. Such factors undoubtedly have an effect but they do not tell the whole story. Consider that the descendants of Sutton Hoo's people ruled the world in a later period, when the grandeur and power of ancient Egypt had crumbled away to nothing. Hence the explanation is not in material advantages alone, but in these plus many cultural factors that determine the achievement and vigor of peoples in a given time and place. The factors leading to conservatism are complex and much remains to be learned about them. One persistent influence is a reluctance to change a pattern that works. If the basic adaptations of a people are meeting their needs, they are less apt to experiment with change than when a crisis appears. This reluctance is shown in the archaeological record by the many prehistoric groups who developed a reasonably secure hunting and gathering existence but never developed agriculture. Such close adaptation to environment, providing a kind of security but at the same time setting limits on population growth and other change, is seen in the survival of "Mesolithic" kinds of communities and the characteristic shell middens which mark their archaeological remains.

EXTREME MARGINAL COMMUNITIES:
SHELL-MIDDEN DWELLERS

Although Sutton Hoo is an example of a marginal-culture monument, even more remote marginality can be seen in the sites where shell-midden peoples lived. Shell middens are simply the remains of villages and camps left by people who depend upon shellfish for a large part of their diet. Since mussels, clams, and oysters are generally available throughout the year, the peoples who learned to gather and utilize these foods had a relatively dependable food supply which could be counted upon at all seasons. In contrast, most hunters and gatherers are subject to seasonal variability in the abundance of food — a "feast or famine" situation. Once having worked out the adaptation to a coastal environment, shell-midden peoples were often content to continue with their way of making a living after other peoples around them had developed new and more efficient ways. The oldest remains of shell-midden peoples were left in the Mesolithic period of the Old World, about 8,000 to 10,000 years ago, when Upper Paleolithic man turned to small game and marine foods as the large Pleistocene animals became extinct. A similar change seems to have taken place at about the same time in the New World, and many shell middens in the New World are over 7,000 years old.

This ancient adaptation to marine resources in the gathering of shellfish persisted until recent times. What was once a new cultural adaptation to environment came to be a way of life for many marginal cultures which retained this subsistence method while most other peoples went on to develop farming and animal breeding, with the richer elaborations of culture that go with them. A few shell-midden cultures have survived until the present in remote coastal areas.

Shell middens border all the oceans of the world and extend inland for hundreds of miles along major river courses. They exist in uncounted numbers, more than 400 being recorded for the shores of San Francisco Bay alone. Shell middens are primarily accumulations of kitchen refuse and are frequently called "kitchen middens." But most shell middens contain much more than the refuse of food preparation, the additional objects deriving from a common practice of living atop the analog of the city dump. Although shell middens are artificial accumulations, they are for the most part unintentional and occur because of the untidy household habit of throwing refuse out the door rather than carting it off to a distance.

With the passage of time (and not necessarily a long time), the increasing accumulation of debris that forms a shell midden may build up to an appreciable hill, attaining a height of 30 feet or more and an area of several acres. Shell middens accumulate at a more rapid rate than other kinds of archaeological sites that lack the bulk refuse represented by cast-off shells.

In the Old World, shell middens accumulated in some numbers about 10,000 years ago around the shores of the Baltic, then a huge freshwater lake inhabited by great numbers of fish and a kind of shellfish called *Ancylus;* for this reason it is often called the Ancylus Sea. Several writers have proposed that the big-game hunters of the Upper Paleolithic period were so efficient that they forced their quarry to extinction. In addition, the changing climate and vegetation drew the surviving game animals northward. The theory suggests that European peoples then turned to the resources of the Ancylus Sea and began to depend on fishing and shellfish collecting. For whatever cause, the change did take place, and the first shell middens mark the transition from the Upper Paleolithic to the Mesolithic cultural development.

The wide distribution of shell middens, ancient and recent, show that cultures of a generally Mesolithic appearance have occurred all over the world wherever a coastline affords the required environmental conditions. In some areas, the gathering of shells was only a supplement to other hunting activities, or even to early agriculture, but in other areas shellfish appear to have provided the staple food.

THE DRAKES BAY MIDDEN

One of the smallest and simplest sites of a shell-midden culture was a small village on the shores of Drakes Bay in California, about thirty miles north of San Francisco. The physical remains of the village consist of a shell midden about 50 feet in diameter and 3 feet deep, near a small spring of fresh water which flows onto the beach. When occupied, the village probably had no more than three little brush houses and a population of perhaps 15. Somewhat larger villages were situated close by, and this one may have been related somehow to a larger community. An archaeological find of this kind could hardly be less impressive; yet it has significance for understanding the course of man's development.

Although the Drakes Bay village was occupied in the sixteenth century and is therefore recent in world history, it was still in the

Fig. 64. The Drakes Bay site, California. *The whole extent of the village was less than the small area in this photograph.*

Fig. 65. Iron rods from the Drakes Bay site. *These rods, an inch in diameter and four feet long, may have come from a galleon shipwrecked in 1595. They were carried to the archaeological site by the Indians but apparently not used by them for anything.*

138

Fig. 67. Pieces of a large Oriental stoneware jar from the Drakes Bay site. *Identified as sixteenth-century in date, these pieces are among the historic artifacts which served as time markers for the site.*

prehistoric period for its part of the world. Northern California had no native recorders of history and had not yet been explored or settled by Europeans. But though an archaeologist usually has difficulty assigning precise dates to sites even this recent along the west coast of the United States, the dating of the Drakes Bay midden is precisely known through a historical accident. In 1595 a Spanish galleon under command of Sebastián Rodríguez Cermeño put into Drakes Bay, and the Spanish visited the Indian villages. The galleon was wrecked by a storm and the Spanish were forced to make their way to Mexico in a small open boat. Remains of the wreck were soon picked up by the Indians and found their way into the shell-midden village, to become very precise time markers for archaeologists in 1949-1953. The most diagnostic dating finds are many pieces of blue and white Chinese porcelain of the Ming dynasty. Dishes and bowls were part of the ship's cargo, being carried from the Philippines to Mexico for sale. In the shipwreck, the broken porcelain became scattered on the beach where pieces of it were picked up and carried home as curiosities by the Indians. A few of the Indians even experimented with the pieces by chipping flakes from the edges to make rude scrapers, but for the most part the fragments were discarded and became part of the refuse composing the midden.

Pieces of a large oriental stoneware jar were also found in the site, at a deeper and accordingly earlier level than the porcelain fragments. The origin of these is not known, but it is a plausible guess that they were derived from the 1579 visit of Sir Francis Drake, the only known European to visit this coast before Cermeño. In any case, the village can be assigned to the late sixteenth century, and the shallowness of the deposit indicates that it was not occupied for very long.

TABLE 7. CHRONOLOGY OF THE CENTRAL CALIFORNIA COAST

The cultures were those of shell-midden peoples throughout. The separation of different periods as named on the chart is based on differences in the style of artifacts rather than on basic differences in culture.

Date	Event
1780 A.D.	Spanish occupation
1500 A.D.	Drakes Bay; 16th-century sites
1000 A.D.	Late Coast
500 A.D.	Middle Central California Coast

The site was excavated by the University of California between 1949 and 1953. Because it is a small midden, almost the whole site has been systematically examined. Most excavations are based on a very small fragment of a site, often less than one per cent of the total volume, but the objects found at the Drakes Bay midden represent almost everything there rather than a random sample.

Despite the recent date of the site (the New World had been discovered by Europeans a scant century earlier and Elizabeth I was on the throne of England), the people of the Drakes Bay village had an essentially Mesolithic economy. Their living came from hunting and gathering the resources of the region, the most reliable of which came out of the bay and the ocean. Shell middens are by their very nature informative regarding the subsistence techniques of the peoples who made them. The sites are composed largely of actual food remains and they therefore tell not only what things were being eaten but also the relative importance of the food resources represented in the refuse. For the Drakes Bay village, food remains included the following:

1. Shell, primarily *Saxidomus,* a large clam extensively sought by modern sportsmen.
2. Crab shells and claws representing gathering of crabs from the shallow waters adjacent to the site. No artifacts were found that suggest how the crabs were caught.
3. Bones of sea mammals (seals, sea lions, and sea otters) and of occasional land animals like deer. Some of these were hunted with bow and arrow, judging from stone arrow points found in the midden; some were probably also killed with clubs, especially the sea animals that were relatively slow moving when on the beaches.
4. Bird bones, including more than 2,000 individual bones representing about 30 species of birds, primarily waterfowl such as ducks and geese. They must represent a major part of the hunting activities of the people. Presumably the birds were hunted with bow and arrow. Traps, snares, and nets may also have been used, but no physical remains of them have been found.

Plant foods have not been preserved and their presence is suggested to archaeologists only by a few stone mortars and pestles for grinding seeds. The Spanish account of the 1595 visit men-

Fig. 69. Pestle from the Drakes Bay site. *Used with a stone mortar to grind wild plant seeds, this was a basic tool in the environmental adaptation of the hunting and gathering Indians of Drakes Bay. Its length is 7 inches (Compare Figs. 40 and 80.)*

Fig. 70. Bone and antler implements representing the standard tools of the Drakes Bay site. *At the bottom are three awls used in basket making; the two tools at upper left are flakers used in chipping obsidian arrow points, and the tool at upper right is a wrench used for straightening arrow shafts (length 7½ inches). Such tools are part of the standard inventory of many hunting and gathering peoples and quite similar items occur from Upper Paleolithic sites in Europe. (Compare Fig. 21 and others.)*

142

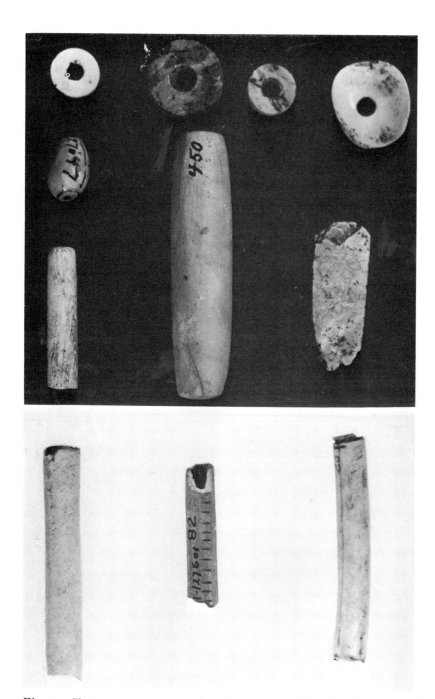

Fig. 72. Shell ornaments (upper) and tubular bird-bone beads (lower) from the Drakes Bay site. *These represent the total collection of ornaments from the site and exemplify the limited time for aesthetic accomplishment in the hunting and gathering society. The largest shell bead is ½ inch in diameter; the length of the shortest bone tube is 2 inches.*

tions that the people used grass seeds for food, and they must have utilized other seasonal plant foods, but apparently meat and shellfish resources were most important. The Drakes Bay environment afforded a reasonably secure living for its few families, yet resources were not abundant enough to permit great expansion of the population. For hundreds, perhaps thousands, of years the Drakes Bay coast was settled by small villages supported by land and ocean resources. Interestingly enough, fish were caught, but other marine resources, particularly shellfish, were more important. Improved fishing techniques could have led to a big increase in the population.

The shell-midden people at Drakes Bay needed little in the way of technological equipment for house building and the like, and they had a minimum of material goods. Their houses were simple brush huts partly covered with earth, their clothing a loin cloth for men and a skirt of skin or rushes for women. These facts are known from Spanish accounts, there is no direct archaeological evidence. The Indians at the Drakes Bay village used baskets as containers for carrying and cooking (they had no pottery) and their household equipment was of the simplest. They made stone arrowpoints and scraping tools and a variety of small implements of bone. Thus the Drakes Bay population had an extremely simple technology. Even their equipment of exploiting the sea was limited, since they had no specialized fishing gear and no boats except a *balsa* of rushes, useable only in sheltered water.

A small and scattered population like that of Drakes Bay is not likely to develop complex means of social control. In the archaeological evidence there is no indication of social classes or of the superiority of one person over another. The people had chiefs, according to Spanish accounts, but these were individuals with limited authority. We may infer that the people were democratic, with everyone pretty much on a par with his neighbor. The clues of social cleavage demonstrated by Ur, in Egypt, and at the Sutton Hoo ship burial are lacking from the Drakes Bay remains. Organized warfare, community building projects, and ideas of a "state" must have been entirely absent.

Most of the individual's time was demanded for the food quest, and there is no indication that the Drakes Bay people attempted to accumulate a surplus and store it for future use. The sea food that was available the year around would keep such people going so that they were never forced to think of the future nor to plan for long seasons of scarcity. Although they were not likely to starve, they did not accumulate enough food to let them quit working for a period of time. In consequence, such leisure activities as artistic endeavors are virtually unrepresented in the archaeological collections. The people made a few simple kinds of shell beads for personal adornment, and presumably found an outlet for aesthetic impulses in the manufacture of baskets and feather ornaments, but this activity is close to the minimum of its kind for human societies.

Even though a site lacks elaborate material objects, it is possible for a people to have had complex ideas of religion, social organization, and the like. These aspects of culture are among the most difficult to infer from archaeology, particularly from simple remains like those found at Drakes Bay. Yet a few bits of evidence have been found. The Drakes Bay group made stone pendants called charmstones that were used in historic times as good-luck fetishes for hunting and fishing; presumably the archaeological examples had the same meaning. The Drakes Bay people also buried their dead with simple offerings of tools, so they may have wanted to provide for the dead in an afterworld. The beliefs of the group may have been far more complex than we can infer from our meager archaeological evidence, yet we must suppose that the little leisure and small population prevented development of an organized priesthood, of temple structures, and of religious activities requiring many man-hours of effort.

Summary

To summarize: The Sutton Hoo ship burial, even with its impressive offerings, is an example of one kind of marginality; in terms of world developments it typifies the fringes of civilization. The little village at Drakes Bay is an extreme case of the same thing, for the Drakes Bay villagers were almost entirely outside of world developments. Yet in neither case can it be said that the people stagnated. Both groups had developed features that gave them a distinctive identity so that they were far more than mere shadows of older cultures. It is only in the broad comparative sense that these cultures can be seen as "primitive."

SELECTED REFERENCES

The references below (aside from Green 1963) are the original site reports dealing with the discoveries discussed in this chapter.

SUTTON HOO

BRUCE-MITFORD, R. L. S.
  1947   *The Sutton Hoo Ship Burial, a Provisional Guide.* British Museum, London.

GREEN, CHARLES
  1963   *Sutton Hoo. The Excavation of a Royal Ship Burial.* Merlin Press, London.

PHILLIPS, C. W.
  1956   The Excavation of the Sutton Hoo Ship Burial. *Recent Archaeological Excavations in Britain* (R. L. S. Bruce-Mitford, editor), pp. 145-166. Macmillan Company, New York.

DRAKES BAY

HEIZER, R. F.
  1941   Archaeological Evidence of Sebastián Rodríguez Cermeño's California Visit in 1595. *California Historical Society Quarterly*, Vol. 20, No. 4 (also published separately as a pamphlet). San Francisco.

MEIGHAN, CLEMENT W., and R. F. HEIZER
  1953   Archaeological Exploration of 16th Century Indian Mounds at Drakes Bay. In *The Plate of Brass*, California Historical Society Special Publication No. 25, pp. 73-81. San Francisco.

⑧ NEW WORLD MAN IN THE PALEOLITHIC STAGE

The New World, like the old, had its shell-midden dwellers, its gatherers, farmers, and civilizations. It shared in the general evolution of man's culture, but by reason of isolation from Old World centers followed its own path of development. Archaeological sites that date from the beginnings of culture in the New World, like the Lehner site to be discussed, show the cultural base upon which the aboriginal peoples of the New World developed their later adaptation. Sites of this kind are also important in comparing the Old and New World paths of development.

North and South America can be referred to as a New World not only in terms of western history but also in terms of the history of humanity. All scholars are agreed that man originated in the Old World and came to the New World at some relatively recent date. This conclusion rests largely on negative evidence, namely that no extremely ancient human forms or human cultures have been discovered in the New World. This is not conclusive, and most of the discoveries of ancient man in the New World have yet to be made. However, the extensive explorations that have been carried on, particularly in North America, make it unlikely that archaeologists would have failed to discover fossil human forms and very ancient cultures if they were present. In point of fact, not only are there no fossil humans in the New World comparable to the Australopithecinae or to Peking man, but there are

147

none of the fossil primate ancestors from which these or similar forms have developed. Hence it seems quite certain that man's biological and cultural origins lie somewhere in the Old World and that during the first phases of man's development the New World was uninhabited by humans.

The route by which man entered the New World is generally agreed to have been across the Bering Strait between Siberia and Alaska. This is the only point at which the two continents are in close proximity and the only place where people with simple technologies could make a crossing. Even today one can cross the Bering Strait in a kayak without ever being out of sight of land (there are small islands in the middle) and in the past it is likely that the strait was even narrower than it is today. In the winter, with such a strait frozen over, man could have walked across from the Old World to the New.

The date when man first entered the New World is still uncertain. Until about 1924, it was believed that no humans had occupied the New World until the last few thousand years. But in 1924, an important discovery at Folsom, Colorado, indicated that humans lived in the New World at the same time as large animals now extinct (the same kind of discovery that confirmed the antiquity of man in the Old World). This famous find consisted of the bones of an extinct form of giant bison among which were found stone spear points of unquestionably human manufacture. After this discovery, archaeologists began a more intensive search for ancient human remains, and there are now many discoveries of artifacts associated with the bones of extinct animals in the New World. One of these is discussed below.

With the development of the radiocarbon dating method it became possible to establish New World dates. Although dating problems are still a matter of dispute, there is now much evidence for human occupation ten to eleven thousand years ago in North America. Man was widely dispersed through the New World by that time, and we must estimate the first entry of man into the New World as at least 20,000 years ago. A few radiocarbon dates in the 20,000-to-30,000-year time range may be associated with human activity, but finds of this antiquity are either doubtful or very skimpy (single artifacts or bones, charcoal) so that they permit little in the way of cultural reconstruction. Whether or not these finds are verified, they have little to offer to the present discussion. We know man was in the New World by 10,000 years ago, and we think man was in the New World considerably before that date. However, even the most extreme estimates place man's existence in the New World as quite late in the total time that man has existed on earth. Nevertheless, humans entering the New World 10,000 years ago must have been on an exceedingly simple level of development — something comparable to the Upper Paleolithic, or at most the Mesolithic cultures of the Old World.

Evidence for what might be called "Lower Paleolithic Man" in the New World is less clear. There are sites which yield a large number, sometimes a predominance, of very crude stone tools. In Southern California, for example, assemblages of tools are found the majority of which are in the chopper tradition not too different in form and manufacture from tools like those found in the Peking cave. However, these same sites include grinding stones and chipped stone points, as well as a few polished objects, all of them evidence of a later technological stage. In addition, some sites have been dated by radiocarbon at only 7,000 years in age and it must be concluded that the very crude stone tools represent a persistence of older tool techniques. This confusion points up a fact always to be borne in mind by the archaeologist, namely that a crude and simple technology does not of itself indicate great age, nor do crude remains prove a simple technology — for example, quarry sites where stone tool manufacture was carried out may be strewn with the coarsest of chipped stones where artifacts were "roughed out" and then carried away to be finished elsewhere. What first looks like an ancient site may be only a workshop for an advanced society.

There are some interesting differences between the big-game hunter sites of the New World and those of the Old World. First, the New World has yielded nothing comparable to the magnificent cave paintings found in Old World Upper Paleolithic sites. These paintings, so far as we know, are restricted to western Europe and have not been found in other areas of Upper Paleolithic occupation such as Asia. A second difference is that the New World sites are primarily locations where animals were killed or butchered, rather than dwelling sites. As a result, physical evidence for the earliest hunters of the New World is almost nonexistent, and no sites are known in which human skeletons are found in direct association with stone tools and the remains of food resources. In the Old World, on the other hand, the Upper Paleolithic sites tend to be occupation areas rather than sites of animal kills. The suggestion from this comparison is that the dwelling places of the New World big-game hunters have yet to be discovered. We can anticipate that such finds will be made within the next few years, and that much additional light will be thrown on the earliest humans in the New World. Meanwhile, we must be content with such fragmentary records of these early hunters as are given by the site discussed below.

THE LEHNER SITE

Human remains in association with the bones of fossil animals are now known in sites from subarctic North America to the southern tip of South America, and it now takes a sizeable book to describe all of the discoveries that have been made. As techniques of excavation and dating were improved, later finds have generally been recorded with greater detail and accuracy than the older ones. A good example is the Lehner mammoth site, a model excavation that shows how such remains are discovered and reported in the New World.

The Lehner site is in the southeastern Arizona desert only a few miles north of the Mexican border. The desert is cut by arroyos that remain dry for most of the year but carry flood waters during periods of rainfall. Such gullies with their ever-crumbling banks, repeatedly cut by flooding, have been important in archaeological discoveries in the arid West, where bones, hearths, and stone tools are often revealed. Just such a discovery was made by E. F. Lehner, a rancher and owner of the site, who observed a number of animal bones embedded in a gully bank about eight feet below the desert surface. Lehner called his discovery to the attention of the University of Arizona. After heavy rains in 1955 exposed still more bones, exploratory excavations were begun under the direction of E. W. Haury of the University of Arizona.

Initially there was no evidence of human occupation, but the site was excavated because the bones were those of mammoth, and the geology indicated that the mammoth had lived recently enough that human remains might be encountered. This was a fortunate decision; tools were soon found associated with the bones of many animals, all in an undisturbed situation where their exact relationships could be established.

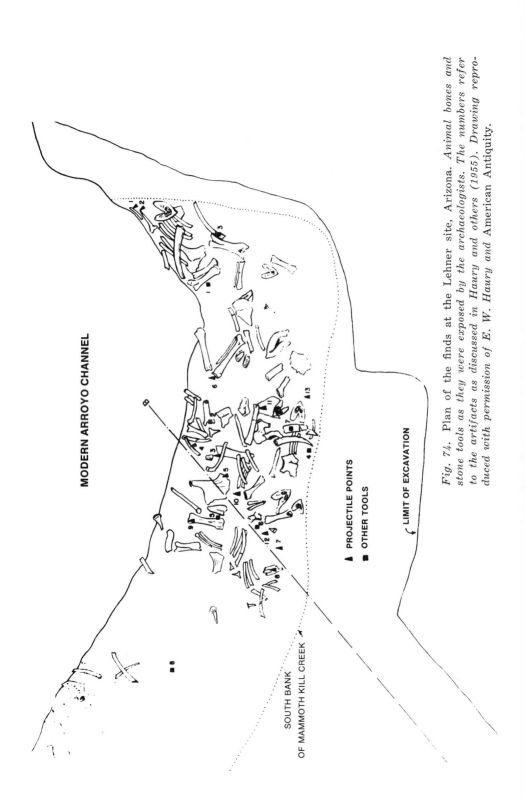

MODERN ARROYO CHANNEL

▲ PROJECTILE POINTS

■ OTHER TOOLS

↙ LIMIT OF EXCAVATION

SOUTH BANK
OF MAMMOTH KILL CREEK ↗

Fig. 74. Plan of the finds at the Lehner site, Arizona. *Animal bones and stone tools as they were exposed by the archaeologists. The numbers refer to the artifacts as discussed in Haury and others (1955). Drawing reproduced with permission of E. W. Haury and American Antiquity.*

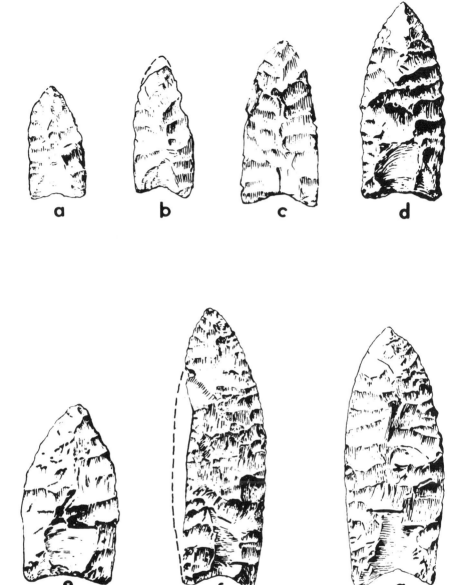

Fig. 75. The collection of 13 Clovis fluted points from the Lehner site. *The drawings are the actual size of the objects. Points of this type are found from several locations of early man in North America. Examples A, B, and C are of transparent quartz; the others are flint. The form and workmanship are quite uniform although the points differ in size. Archaeologists infer, from the size of a point, whether it was probably used on a bow-shot arrow or on a spear — or had some other use. Drawings reproduced with permission of E. W. Haury from* American Antiquity.

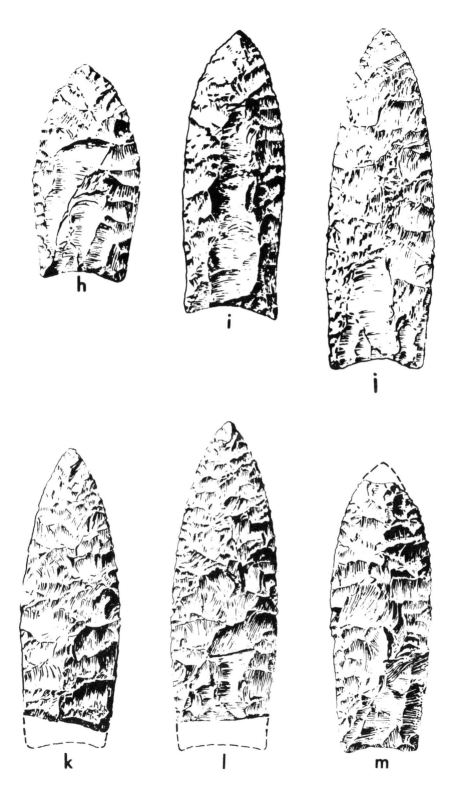

h

i

j

k

l

m

153

To excavate the site, some ten feet of overburden was removed by power machinery, uncovering a bed in which lay the remains of nine mammoths as well as bones of fossil horse, bison, and tapir. Abundant cultural evidence was also present in the form of thirteen stone spearpoints, eight tools for cutting and scraping, and two hearths where the animals were cooked. This is clearly a location where prehistoric hunters killed, butchered and cooked the large mammoths of the terminal Pleistocene period.

Several radiocarbon measurements on charcoal from the hearths dated the site between 11,000 and 12,000 years ago. However, geological evidence suggests the site to be somewhat older, and Haury believes it is at least 13,000 years in age. Although older sites in the New World are known, they are mostly of limited yield, often only a single artifact or fireplace. The Lehner site represents one of the oldest New World assemblages of stone tools found in association with the animals hunted.

The chipped stone points from the Lehner site are distinctive in size and in having a fluting of the base. These points, rather larger than arrowheads, were used to tip small spears. Closely similar points had been found at many other localities in North America, from one of which (Clovis, New Mexico) they have been named Clovis points. Their uniform manufacture over a relatively large area indicates a widespread group of big-game hunters culturally much like the Upper Paleolithic hunters of Europe and the Old World.

A few other simple artifacts, including crude knives and scrapers, were found at the Lehner site and in association with Clovis points at a few other locations. The assemblage of tools has been called the Llano Complex, believed to represent the material culture of a distinctive group of hunters who specialized in elephant hunting. On present evidence, however, this is rather tenuous classification since the meager and widely scattered finds do not yield a full picture of even the material objects used by the makers of Clovis points, and other aspects of their life are completely unknown.

A significant gap in the reconstruction of this ancient period is the absence of human bones. No human skeletal remains that can be positively associated with the flint points have yet been found. This lack is an interesting contrast to the Old World situation, where many skeletons of this age have been found. Either the

New World population was very much smaller at this time, so that skeletons would be less likely to be found, or perhaps the New World people did not dispose of their dead by burial. If the dead were exposed, as they are by some primitive peoples, the chances of encountering a preserved skeleton are much diminished.

In their adaptation to their environment, the ancient big-game hunters of North America must have been similar to the people of the Upper Paleolithic in Europe. Their societies were presumably organized into small traveling bands with a minimum of formal chieftainship and social classes. As to the third important aspect of culture, satisfaction of the "inner man," there is no clue in the limited finds from the Lehner site. The delicate and careful chipping of the projectile points may be noted, but except for this, little of aesthetic quality can be reconstructed.

There is a hint of ceremonialism in the collection of projectile points in that three of the points are much smaller than the others and are made of crystal-clear quartz instead of the flint characteristically used. Transparent crystals, often quartz, are known to have great magical significance for many primitive people, and objects made of this material characteristically are believed to have special potency. The small quartz Clovis points (the only ones ever found of this material) may have represented a kind of "magic bullet" more valued in a supernatural sense than for the physical damage it might inflict.

Nothing has been found in the New World comparable to the cave paintings, elaborately carved bone tools, and similar aesthetic manifestations of 10,000 to 15,000 years ago in Europe. Since no graves have been found either, nothing can be said about the religious beliefs of these ancient people. The discovery that will illuminate these aspects of their culture remains to be made, but we can be sure that it awaits the archaeologist.

Selected References

Haury, E. W., E. B. Sayles, and W. W. Wasley

1959   The Lehner Mammoth Site, Southeastern Arizona. *American Antiquity*, Vol. 25, No. 1, pp. 2-30. Salt Lake City. The site report describing the finds at the Lehner site.

SELLARDS, E. H.
1952   *Early Man in America: A Study in Prehistory.* University of
Texas Press, Austin. A general survey of early-man finds in America.

WORMINGTON, H. M.
1957   *Ancient Man in North America.* Denver Museum of Natural
History, Popular Series No. 4 (Fourth Edition), Denver. The most detailed
general summary available discussing early human sites in the New World.
Recommended volume for those interested in finds like the Lehner site.

⑨ PREHISTORIC NEW WORLD FARMERS

Just as the New World had its hunters comparable to the Old World peoples, so there developed in the New World simple farmers and relatively advanced civilizations. Most, if not all, of these developments seem to have taken place as indigenous developments, for convincing evidence of contacts between Old World and New World peoples is lacking or meager. The New World experienced its own "Neolithic revolution," using different food plants and showing distinctive changes. But as in the Old World, the introduction of agriculture led to greater stability of population and development of social and philosophical areas of human life.

The beginnings of agriculture are poorly known in both the Old World and the New World, since incipient agriculture leaves little evidence for the archaeologist. Only when developed agriculture is present are the effects of producing food through farming clearly seen.

Many New World sites have been excavated that display the early stage of development, in the Eastern and Southwestern United States, throughout Mexico and Central America, and into the Andean region of South America. These sites include major cities, comparable in complexity to the site of Ur, and small hamlets of only a few families. Such sites flourished over time preceding the Christian era until the first European exploration in the sixteenth century and later.

THE PARAGONAH SITE

The archaeological site of Paragonah, named after the town of the same name in southern Utah, is the remains of one of the simpler kinds of farming communities, representative of a Neolithic state of development. Paragonah is a good example of a simple level of agriculture, comparable in its complexity to the sort of culture from which civilizations developed.

Paragonah is one of many known sites representing prehistoric Indian farming communities in Utah; they are found as far north as the Salt Lake City area and westward just into Nevada. This site was occupied between about 900 and 1150 A.D. In the history of the development of agriculture, Paragonah is a marginal community. It appears, like other Indian settlements in Utah, to have been established by colonists who had moved northward and raised corn, beans, and squash on the fringes of the Great Basin deserts.

The environment was not favorable to agriculture, since the country is dry and the least rainfall failure was serious to farmers. Whatever the cause, Paragonah and the sites like it in that area were abandoned in the twelfth century. What happened to the people is not known, but they probably returned to the south and continued farming in more favorable regions.

Paragonah was discovered and excavated in the 1880's by early Mormon pioneers who dug into some of the mounds in search of treasure. The first scientific work was done by Neil M. Judd for the Smithsonian Institution, from 1916 to 1918. Judd excavated the largest mound of the many at the site and gained information about adobe architecture. Subsequently, Paragonah was excavated for seven summer seasons (1954–1961) by field classes from the University of California, Los Angeles.

Most of the site has been destroyed by nearly a century of modern agricultural activity. However, from early accounts, excavations, and mapping of surface remains, it can be inferred that the site originally consisted of approximately 400 small mounds, some only a few feet in diameter and a foot or so in height, the largest 200 feet in diameter and 10 feet high. Each of these separate mounds was the result of accumulating refuse and fallen adobe structures. When occupied, each mound had on top of it one or more small adobe buildings; many mounds had only a single one-room structure but the largest had about sixty buildings of this sort on its summit. Earlier investigators believed these build-

Fig. 77. Model of an abode-walled granary from Paragonah, Utah. *One wall is removed to show the internal features. These small structures, apparently only a few feet high, served to store the agricultural crop and evidence the accumulation of a food surplus by farming peoples.*

Fig. 78. Excavated pit house at the Paragonah site. *See Fig. 79 (color) for a reconstruction of what these houses looked like when complete and in use. The strings lay out the 5-foot squares which were the units of excavation and mapping.*

ings to be houses, but recent work has shown that they were granaries, intended to store corn and other food supplies. Because the dwellings were pit houses located on the flatland between the mounds, they were not found by earlier workers and were not known in detail until the work in the 1950's.

Most of the Paragonah mounds are concentrated in an area about a quarter of a mile square, but outlying scattered remains are found within a square mile. The site represents a major community of its period for the Southwest. Unfortunately, it is difficult to estimate how many people lived in the town. It is certain that not all of the mounds and structures were in use simultaneously, yet the population could hardly have been less than four or five hundred, and perhaps many more occupied the community at its height.

Material objects for archaeological analysis have been found on the floors of the pit houses, some of them with burials. The biggest collection from the site is at the University of California, Los Angeles, with something over 10,000 catalog entries. It includes quantities of pottery, examples of most of the domestic implements used by the people, and specimens of the food crops, preserved in charred form. Some of the houses had burned when the town was occupied; these houses are valuable archaeologically because they contain pieces of carbonized basketry, wooden objects, and otherwise perishable goods not usually preserved in an open site.

Although the people of Paragonah were farmers, their agriculture was simple in comparison with that of the more complex civilizations of Mexico and Central and South America. The people of Paragonah made their living primarily from the basic American crops of corn (maize), beans, and squash. They lived on an alluvial fan at the base of steep red hills, out of which many small creeks flowed across the plain. Possibly they made use of simple irrigation; there is no archaeological evidence. The corn represented in the archaeological collections by carbonized kernels and cobs is a primitive variety with small ears only four or five inches long. Carbonized beans and squash have also been found.

Despite dependence on agriculture, the Paragonah people had not entirely abandoned an older hunting and gathering tradition. Fairly extensive hunting, mostly for deer, was practiced. The relative importance of hunting versus agriculture can only be guessed

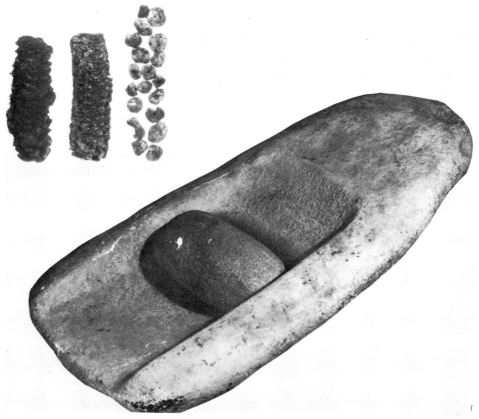

Fig. 80. Milling stone and carbonized cobs and kernels of corn, from Paragonah. *These finds represent the basic corn agriculture which supported the
community. (Compare Figs. 40 and 69.)*

at, but since thousands of animal bones have been found at the
site it seems that hunting contributed a substantial part of the
diet — perhaps as much as half. Such dependence on hunting is
not possible in a developed agricultural economy, for dense populations usually deplete the game resources to the point where
game can furnish only a small supplement to the diet.

The Paragonah people had solved their subsistence problems
reasonably well and had seasonal surpluses of food, as is shown
by the many small adobe granaries or storage rooms for the
annual crop. These rectangular rooms were entered by a hole in
the roof, ordinarily sealed with a piece of sandstone similar to a

Fig. 82. Pottery vessels from Paragonah. *Note the reassembling of broken pieces — a normal part of archaeologists' work. Such fragments are often dispersed over considerable distances.*

Fig. 83. Bone gaming pieces from Paragonah. *Always marked differently on the two sides (the plain ones are usually painted red on one side), these are believed to have been used in some sort of gambling game. The smallest piece is just under an inch long; others are to the same scale. (Compare Fig. 51.)*

manhole cover in size and shape. Occasionally domestic tools were stored in the adobe buildings, but generally they contain no trace of living activity.

The dwellings of the community are simple, follow a definite plan, and show only small variations. The average house was a pit about 12 to 15 feet square, dug into the ground about three feet and then roofed over and covered with earth. These had one room, with a clay-rimmed hearth in the center, and were entered by a ladder through a roof opening. Domestic furnishings were simple: stone grinding tools for preparing corn, baskets and pots for containers and cooking, and probably mats to sleep on. The people lived above a subsistence level and had sufficient food to allow some leisure time. Recreational activities are indicated by common gaming pieces made of bone (similar to dice) and also by stone balls about the size of a golf ball.

The ancient town of Paragonah was far simpler than the urban centers of the Old World previously discussed (Ur and ancient Egypt), yet it had enough people to require organization of social life. The pattern of life in Paragonah is shown in several archaeological features. First, the community itself was more or less planned. All of the houses were oriented in the same direction, and although there were no streets and city blocks, there was a plaza arrangement in the center. There is also evidence that several families (or perhaps one large group of relatives) worked together, for there is only one small storage structure for every five or six pit houses. Apparently several households maintained their food in a common building, and perhaps also shared the land and the agricultural work. The larger storehouses, built around the central plaza, may have been for the food surplus set aside for community leaders or religious personages.

The people had social contacts outside the town, journeying to trade with other farming communities of the same kind within one of two hundred miles. Occasional sherds of foreign pottery found at Paragonah show trade and contact with surrounding regions. The uniformity of these Utah communities shows that they were in fairly close contact. It was far more difficult to meet with peoples to the south, since this involved crossing a greater distance and overcoming several geographic barriers, including the Grand Canyon. As a result, the Utah agriculturalists remained peripheral to cultural developments in the Southwest, and their culture shows slower change than the Southwest proper. The general picture suggests that the Paragonah people were members of a marginal tribe with a certain amount of internal unity but relatively isolated from other peoples of the same type.

The archaeological finds do not show warfare. Such conflict can usually be recognized archaeologically through abundant weapons, defensive constructions, and sometimes human skeletons bearing the marks of injuries from arrow points and clubs. Although some conflict and raiding must have taken place, this agricultural settlement was a relatively peaceful community. This peace is surprising since Paragonah and other aboriginal towns like it were surrounded by desert nomads of different type culturally. Indeed, some writers have suggested that the abandonment of sites like Paragonah (in the twelfth century) was due to pressure from the nomadic desert dwellers who drove out the settled farmers. Yet there is no evidence of palisades or other defensive features at Paragonah nor is the town situated for defense. Apparently the population at Paragonah was able to maintain itself politically by sheer weight of numbers, having many more people than an individual desert band that might challenge them.

As is usual, religious activities are difficult to interpret from archaeological evidence, but there are a few indications that the Paragonah people shared in the sort of southwestern religion practiced today by modern Pueblo Indians. One structure at Paragonah is interpreted as a kiva, the semisubterranean sacred men's house characteristic of the southwest since about 500 A.D. There are more specific indications in the funeral offerings made to a young man found buried under a house floor. His ceremonial costume, similar to that used in modern Pueblo rituals, included animal and bird skins tied to his belt in the back, attested by fragmentary remains of birds and three weasels. Over his body were two batons bearing feathers tied to one end. Such feathered sticks are often carried in the hands of religious performers in present-day ceremonies, and they also wear the small animal skins attached to the belt. Hence the religious pattern of ancient Paragonah, like that of the modern Pueblo Indians, probably involved rituals for the increase of the crops and a harmonious relationship with weather spirits.

The leisure activities of gambling and playing a game with stone balls have already been mentioned. Some attention to aesthetic

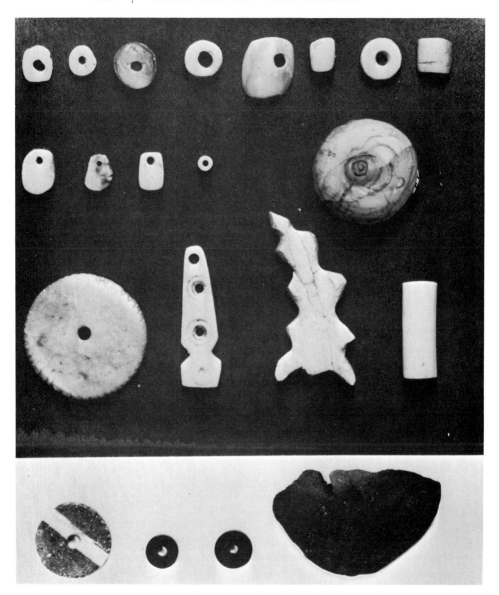

Fig. 85. Ornaments of shell, stone, and bone from Paragonah. *The largest disk is 1¼ inches in diameter; other pieces are the same scale.*

accomplishment is also shown by painted pottery, but this is weakly developed even for the Southwest and looks crude and simple in comparison with the artistic developments of the ancient cities of the Old World. In complexity, Paragonah was a village: small, relatively secure and peaceful, never developing the elaborations characteristic of the simplest city.

Ornaments of shell and stone were found (Fig. 85), also pottery pipes for smoking (Fig. 86, color) ; but like other Paragonah works of art these were simple compared to the products of civilizations.

SELECTED REFERENCES

JENNINGS, JESSE D., AND OTHERS

1956   *The American Southwest: A Problem in Cultural Isolation.* Society for American Archaeology, Memoir No. 11, pp. 59-127. Salt Lake City. Historical development of the archaeological cultures of the American Southwest with particular attention to influences and contacts from other areas.

JUDD, N. M.

1919   *Archaeological Investigations at Paragonah, Utah.* Smithsonian Miscellaneous Collections, Vol. 70, No. 3. Washington. Describes the first archaeological study at Paragonah and excavation of the largest mound at the site.

MEIGHAN, CLEMENT W., AND OTHERS

1956   *Archaeological Investigations in Iron County, Utah.* University of Utah Anthropological Papers, No. 25. Salt Lake City. Report on the 1954 excavations at Paragonah.

WORMINGTON, H. M.

1947   *Prehistoric Indians of the Southwest.* Colorado Museum of Natural History, Popular Series. No. 7. Denver. A summary for the general reader, outlining the sequence of development in the Southwest.

10 CIVILIZATION IN THE NEW WORLD: THE MOCHICA

Some American agriculturalists attained civilizations rivaling the great Bronze Age cities of the Old World. One of the most dynamic of the New World civilizations is that of the Mochica, on the north coast of Peru between 400 and 1000 A.D.

The period of Mochica culture is often referred to as the Florescent Period of New World civilizations, during which many aspects of culture (particularly art and handicrafts) reached a peak of development. The archaeological picture of the Mochica culture is more complete than for most cultures found in many parts of the world because, as in Egypt, remains are preserved by an arid climate and perishable items not usually found in archaeological contexts are recoverable. The reconstruction of Mochica culture is also aided by a unique and elaborate ceramic style including painted and modeled vessels depicting most aspects of Mochica daily life. Unlike the ancient Greeks, who idealized the human form and usually represented it in its most beautiful aspects, the Mochica in their art show all varieties of human form including the ill, the blind, and the maimed. Mochica pottery also depicts plants, animals, and objects of human manufacture. Since there are no written inscriptions in this part of the world, the imperishable representations in pottery are invaluable for cultural reconstruction.

168

Mochica culture was an outgrowth of an earlier period (called Salinar) and indeed archaeologists have recovered evidence for a long sequence of cultures in the Peruvian area (see Table 8). The

TABLE 8. CHRONOLOGY OF THE NORTH COAST OF PERU

This table is modified after Mason (1957).

Date	Event
A.D. 1532	Spanish conquest
1438	Inca
1300	Chimu
1000	Tiahuanaco
400	*Mochica*
	Late Gallinazo
500 B.C.	Salinar
	Early Gallinazo
850 B.C.	Cupisnique
1250 B.C.	Guanape
2550 B.C.	Huaca Prieta (development of early agriculture)

Mochica people expanded their territory, partly at least by military conquest, until at their height they occupied the valleys of six rivers emptying into the Pacific Ocean along the northern coast of Peru. Territory under their control extended over an area of about 1,600 square miles, but only a small portion of this was usable land. Except for the narrow river valleys the area is one of the dryest deserts in the world. The Mochica, like the people of Ur and ancient Egypt, flourished in an arid river valley environment. However, instead of a single major drainage system like the Nile, they had a series of small river valleys.

The Mochica culture was not an isolated development. In its time, comparable Peruvian cultures flourished both to the north and to the south. Far to the north, other aboriginal civilizations flourished in Central America and Mexico, and the Maya civilization of Yucatán was undergoing its florescent development.

Since Mochica remains are found in all the valleys in the territory, it is difficult to choose a type site. However, one of the first investigated Mochica sites, Moche near Trujillo, continues to be scientifically valuable. Moche was explored in 1899 by Max Uhle, a German archaeologist then working for the University of California at Berkeley under the patronage of Phoebe Apperson Hearst. Careful scientific archaeology was the exception rather than the rule in 1899, but Uhle's description of Moche and his

Fig. 87. View of Moche, Peru, from the Cerro Blanco —*the high "white hill."* *The structure in the background is called the Pyramid of the Sun, the one in* *the foreground the Pyramid of the Moon. These modern names do not have* *any verified source in the Mochica culture. Photograph by Christopher Don-* *nan, 1963.*

Fig. 88. Left portion of the Pyramid of the Sun at Moche, from the direc- tion of the Cerro Blanco. *The structure, much eroded, is of mud brick.* *Photograph by Christopher Donnan, 1963.*

Fig. 89. The Pyramid of the Moon at Moche. *In the background is the Cerro Blanco, at the base of which the site of Moche developed. Photograph by Christopher Donnan, 1963.*

Fig. 90. Part of a necklace from cemetery F, Moche. *This work demonstrates the artistry and technological skill of Mochica craftsmen. The individual shells are imitations, carved out of thick pieces of marine shell. Each shell bears a copper cap, now corroded, which once held the suspension ring. The surface was decorated with small disks of turquoise (missing on these examples) set into pits with an adhesive. Each individual shell represents several skills. Individual pieces are about 1½ inches tall.*

discoveries through its excavation were exceptionally thorough and methodical for his time and the results are still important.

The ruins at Moche were described in an early paper by Uhle, and his collections of archaeological material, sent to the University of California, were first described in print by A. L. Kroeber in 1925.

Moche is dominated by the ruins of two very large adobe pyramids, located between the Moche River and a conical peak, Cerro Blanco, about a thousand feet high. The pyramids, the smaller referred to as the Pyramid of the Moon and the larger as the Pyramid of the Sun, are separated by a flat plain some 500 yards long, on which the ancient settlement was situated. The Pyramid of the Sun is the largest pre-Columbian structure in Peru. Resting on a large constructed platform which is itself 60 feet in height, the pyramid is 338 feet square and slightly over 90 feet tall.

Ruins of adobe buildings represent the dwellings of the community, but most of Uhle's archaeological search was for cemetery areas, several of which had been found and looted before his time. Here, as in other regions where elaborate archaeological remains occur, looting of sites has long been a profession of some people, and few of the Mochica specimens in museums or collections were obtained by archaeologists under controlled conditions of study. Uhle was fortunate in finding a burial area (cemetery F) from which he recovered 33 graves intact. His notes and the collection from these graves serve as the primary definition of Mochica culture.

Cemetery F included some burials in the sand, but it also revealed prepared tombs of adobe bricks, roofed with a layer of poles supporting an adobe brick covering. In such tombs, possibly family crypts, were found multiple burials of three to five individuals. Grave offerings consisted primarily of a wide variety of pottery vessels, about 500 of them occurring with the 33 graves. In addition, small objects of gold and copper, stone beads, and shell ornaments were found.

The existence of cities and large constructions during Mochica times shows a stable and efficient adaptation to the environment. As we have seen in the Old World examples, such adaptation was most effectively achieved through agriculture, and New World developments followed the same lines. For the Mochica, agriculture was well established, and over 30 domesticated plants were cultivated; remains of the plants and representations of most of them in pottery have been found. The principal crops were corn, beans, and squash, the basic agricultural plants for most of the New World. Also cultivated were peanuts, potatoes, pumpkins, cucumbers and manioc, as well as plants unfamiliar to most modern farmers such as chirimoyas and lucumas. The crops were irrigated by canals and aqueducts up to 75 miles in length, evidences of engineering as well as agricultural proficiency. Other engineering knowledge among the Mochica is shown by pyramids and plazas such as those at Moche, and by aqueducts and well-made roads that linked the Mochica settlements even though there were no wheeled vehicles. Goods were transported in packs, either by humans or llamas.

The Mochica supplemented their diet by hunting and even more by fishing. Painted and modeled representations on the pottery show deer hunts and a wide variety of marine life. As domestic animals the Mochica had llamas for beasts of burden and guinea pigs for food.

Mochica technology included work in stone, shell, and wood, and a well developed metallurgy in copper, gold, silver, and platinum (but not bronze). Of household arts, the masterful ceramics and intricate textile art make many Mochica specimens prize display pieces of museums.

In America as in the Old World, cities and such large community constructions as irrigation systems, aqueducts, and large temples could not have been developed without community effort and strong supervision. These works, which required many men and often years to complete, are testimonials to strong social control. The Mochica government seems to have been dynastic; that is, held in certain family lines within a class of nobility. It was sustained by religious controls, and the chief civil authorities were also leaders in the religion. Apparently, as in the ancient cities of the Old World, Mochica government operated on the concept that the common man's chief function was to serve the ruling classes who held semi-divine power on earth.

Mochica representations (see Figs. 91-94, color) give abundant evidence of a class of nobility, not only in the form of signs of rank (ear plugs, batons in hand, and elaborate headdresses) but also in paintings of important persons being carried in litters by their servants, councils at which people are seated at the feet of an exalted person (himself on a dais or "throne") and scenes of warriors led by elaborately garbed chiefs. Some insight into the power of the ruling class can be seen in pottery vessels showing mutilated persons, apparently criminals who were punished by facial mutilation or amputation of feet or hands. Similar punitive mutilation is common to many civilizations and occurred in western Europe until relatively recently.

The social position of the common man is not emphasized in the representations, but we see him as a peasant farmer tilling his fields, serving on community efforts such as road building, and serving as a soldier. Such activity implies some degree of public security and some defense against attack by outside enemies. Representations in the arts also indicate that the common man shared the privilege of participating in, or at least observing, religious spectacles through which his leaders placated the gods and insured divine protection for the people. In these details there is a striking similarity between Moche and the Old World's early cities.

The religion of the Mochica apparently centered around a divinity usually represented as a man with large catlike teeth wearing a jaguar headdress. Other deities were also worshiped, including a god of agriculture. It is a plausible surmise that solar and lunar gods were part of the religious belief, although the names for the Pyramids of the Sun and Moon are speculative and not indicated by archaeological evidence. The size of these religious structures shows that the religion must have been complex and impressive, with great community effort required on religious constructions and observances.

The aesthetic achievements of the Mochica are world famous, primarily because of their elaborate and diversified pottery (see figures 91–97, color). As an example of Mochica interest portrayed in ceramics, one Peruvianist (Larco Hoyle) has tabulated the many animals that occur in either modeled or painted form. They include 18 mammals, ranging from bats to bears; 37 birds, 5 reptiles, and 20 molluscs and insects as well as 12 fishes. Although the representations are highly stylized rather than realistic, the key features are often delineated so clearly that one can identify specific kinds of animals. A similar diversity occurs in the representations of plants known and used by the Mochica. Finally humans of all kinds and divine beings are represented in pottery.

The development of higher learning was limited by the absence of a written language, although the Mochica apparently used symbols inscribed on large lima beans as memory devices. These were not writing and could not have served as much more than tallies or reminders of accounts. Whatever the Mochica may have known of mathematics, philosophy, astronomy, and the like can be only guessed at from knowledge of their successors who survived at the time of the Spanish conquest.

The Mochica were only one of several New World cultures meriting the name of civilization. The best known Indian civilizations at the time of Spanish entry into the New World were the Aztec, the Maya, and the Inca. The distinctive Mochica culture had contributed its knowledge to later Peruvian peoples and was extinct. Unfortunately, the Spanish and later European colonists were primarily concerned with controlling and exploiting the New World peoples rather than studying them. A few good accounts of the New World civilizations were written by Europeans who saw these civilizations functioning, but for the most part the New World peoples were submerged in the tide of Old World dominance by Spanish soldiers and settlers, and little record was made of native New World accomplishments. A principal contribution of archaeology is thus to place the New World civilizations in man's history, as a balance and extremely interesting comparison to the more familiar "birth of civilization" in the Old World.

SELECTED REFERENCES

BENNETT, WENDELL C., AND JUNIUS B. BIRD
  1949   *Andean Culture History.* American Museum of Natural History, Handbook Series No. 15. New York. A popular and well-illustrated summary of archaeological developments in the Andean area.

KROEBER, ALFRED L.
  1925   *The Uhle Pottery Collections from Moche.* University of California Publications in American Archaeology and Ethnology, Vol. 21, No. 5, pp. 191-234. Berkeley. The original description of the pottery collected by Uhle at Moche and sent to the University of California.

LARCO HOYLE, RAFAEL
  1938-1939   *Las Mochicas.* 2 vols. Lima.

MASON, J. ALDEN

1957   *The Ancient Civilizations of Peru*. Penguin Books, Harmondsworth. A detailed general work including discussion and illustration of archaeological cultures discovered in Peru.

STEWARD, JULIAN H., editor

1946-1950   *Handbook of South American Indians*. Smithsonian Institution, Bureau of American Ethnology Bulletin 143 (6 vols.), Washington. A massive study summarizing in many articles by individual scholars, the ethnology and archaeology of all South America. Volume 2 is on the Andean region and includes discussion of Mochica culture.

STRONG, WILLIAM D.

1947   *Finding the Tomb of a Warrior God*. National Geographic Magazine, Vol. 91, pp. 453-482. Washington. Popular account of the discovery and study of a rich Mochica burial.

STRONG, WILLIAM D., AND CLIFFORD EVANS, JR.

1952   *Cultural Stratigraphy in the Viru Valley, Northern Peru*. Columbia University Press, New York. Monographic study on the sequences of cultures in one of the northern Peruvian valleys.

UHLE, MAX

1913   Die Ruinen von Moche. *Journal de la Société des Américanistes de Paris*, n.s., Vol. 10, pp. 95-118. Paris.

11 ARCHAEOLOGY AND CULTURE CHANGE

So far in this book we have examined some archaeological sites and seen what kinds of objects were found in them and what kinds of conclusions the archaeologist can draw from his findings. The examples were chosen to give a cross section of archaeological discoveries and to demonstrate that even though the sites and finds are very different in content and complexity, there is a basic approach of value for all of them.

The examples have all been primarily concerned with specific sites having specific artifacts and with the way in which the archaeologist reaches conclusions from the things he finds. How does the archaeologist know? How can he make the statements he does? The examples have presented archaeological interpretation based in part on measuring, in part on inferences drawn from relationships between groups of objects, in part on analogy to the situation among living primitive people, and in part upon written historical records. These various bases show that archaeological interpretation (like most scholarly interpretation) is in part a science, in part an art. When the archaeologist talks about tools and adaptation to the environment, his conclusions usually rest on abundant direct evidence and his method is scientific in his handling of data and conclusions. When the archaeologist talks about social organization, he rarely has direct evidence but must rely on inference based on settlement size, type of dwelling, and other indications. His conclusions are apt to be much less detailed in this aspect of human affairs. When he talks about the religion of ancient peoples, or about the hunting magic in the cave paintings of the Upper Paleolithic, the archaeologist's interpretation is quite indirect and is based on the use of art among recent primitive people. To be sure, the careful scholar will always have a reason for his conclusions, and his explanation may be plausible and quite convincing, but the degrees of *certainty* are not the same when archaeologists draw conclusions about the meaning of cave paintings and when they talk about the construction of a pyramid.

With all these difficulties of interpretation, the analysis of a particular site and the finds made there can nevertheless provide significant knowledge about extinct cultures. Although a complete reconstruction of the lives of past peoples is not possible, much can be drawn even from fragmentary and meager remains. But the examples have been concerned with reconstructing individual cultures, and there is a different level of analysis in which the archaeologist seeks to understand the development of culture in general — not the growth of a single culture but the developing knowledge of mankind as a whole. Having examined a cross-section of archaeological finds and the reconstruction of individual cultures, let us briefly see what archaeologists attempt to do with the over-all picture of culture change.

Even the few examples discussed in this book have displayed parallels between Old and New World, between different civilizations, between hunters in one place and hunters in another. The professional archaeologist, familiar with dozens or hundreds of such examples, is much interested in whether or not there are underlying patterns which show changes in general growth, rather than a series of unrelated individual sequences.

KINDS OF CULTURE CHANGE

Archaeologists — and other scholars including historians, biologists, and other social scientists — have developed detailed studies of particular kinds of change in man's over-all history, among which seven may be mentioned:

1. *Population growth.* The increase in man's numbers since the beginning of humanity.
2. *Change in mobility.* The tendency of people to become more and

more sedentary as their subsistence activities improved and they became able to make a living without moving over the country.

3. *Complexity increases.* In material objects, the development of more things, and more kinds of things, since the simple beginnings of culture. Complexity increase may also be measured in social and religious areas.

4. *Energy utilization.* The progress from man's reliance on his own unaided muscle power through the use of domesticated animals, steam, electricity, and atomic power.

5. *Technological sophistication.* The sequence of Stone, Bronze, and Iron Ages and the ramifications of making ever better implements.

6. *Urbanism and/or complex political developments.* The move to cities and the *tendency* toward more structured government systems.

7. *Changing subsistence and economic patterns.* The change from hunting to agriculture to industrialization.

In addition to such broad-scale studies, there are multitudes of studies depicting cultural change in less universal features of human life and over shorter spans of time. These range from studies of the fluctuation in costume to the effects of introducing steel axes to aborigines. But we are here more concerned with general change for humanity as a whole rather than with the specific examples.

POINTS OF VIEW ON CULTURE CHANGE

In depicting shifts or trends of change through time, archaeologists make use of several simple diagrams representing points of view. These viewpoints are usually implicit rather than explicit. Yet they have a great effect on how prehistory is interpreted, and it is worthwhile to examine some of the diagrammatic ways of showing change. All such schematic charts have two principal disadvantages: first they tend to oversimplify a complex process; and second, the diagram itself sometimes limits the way in which the process of change can be seen. The diagram is like a light filter, transmitting one color and excluding others. An archaeologist who gets too closely attached to a particular scheme as the explanation of events may be unable to recognize other and perhaps better explanations. For present purposes, let us examine

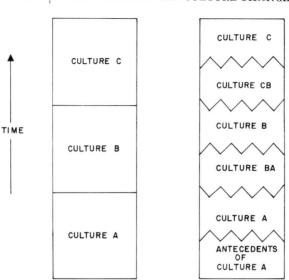

Fig. 98. "Stages" diagrams for presenting culture history. *At left, the standard method of presenting a sequence of cultures or stages of development. Although useful in presenting a quick outline of sequence, such a diagram gives the impression of cultures as discrete entities, like beads on a string which are quite distinct from one another. The "stages" are more faithful to history if they show interlacing phases as the right-hand diagram suggests. Since culture change is a continuum, with each culture very much like its predecessor, the drawing of a "stages" diagram always represents more or less arbitrary decisions about how many stages there are and where the dividing lines are to be drawn.*

Abrupt changes in culture do occur in such cases as invasions, reoccupation of sites after a period of abandonment, and similar events. The levels of an archaeological site then conform to the drastic cultural changes. However, such changes are in a very small minority — most sites reveal a continuum of cultural development.

the different ways in which long-range culture change is traditionally presented, recognizing that there are several ways of looking at the question and that all of them have some advantages and some disadvantages.

There are six principal ways in which cultural development has been portrayed. It is useful in reading archaeological reports to know which pattern the writer had in mind. These are briefly defined as follows:

1. *Cultural "stages."* In this pattern, cultures are a succession

of strata or pigeonholes. This is the most common way of representing culture change — a sequence of named cultures arranged in time. Although the easiest way of describing a sequence of changes, it has two major faults: First, attention is automatically concentrated on the central and "typical" development — on the elements that distinguish one culture from another rather than on the shared features. The consequence is an unsatisfactory picture of continuity, minimizing the forces of tradition and the fact that any culture shares most of its features with that of the immediately preceding people. Second, in dramatizing the differences and emphasizing the breaks, overuse of the "stages" diagram leads to the "catastrophic" viewpoint of culture change, in which change is related to a disaster such as flood, epidemic, or conquest. But most innovation in culture is seldom due to catastrophe; it grows more usually from the practice of each generation making small modifications in the accustomed patterns of doing things. Hence, the "stages" diagram, while useful in descriptive reports, can be misleading if it is seen as an *explanation* of change rather than as a diagrammatic representation.

Another problem is the question of defining stages and the number of stages in a given time span. To put this another way, how big a change is necessary before one recognizes a new "stage"? There is a standing joke that archaeologists, given a new site, always come up with three stages — Early, Middle and Late. So common are these terms in archaeological writing that they tell more about the way archaeologists think than they do about culture change. Why not two stages, or five, or eleven? The stage classification is a product of the archaeologist's mode of describing his material; it is not a picture of the way cultures change.

2. *Revolutions.* A modified and more sophisticated version is that of V. Gordon Childe, whose term "revolutions" indicates the principal idea of change. Childe correctly recognized that certain points in cultural history had profound effects on later developments, and he designated those points as "revolutions" because of their tremendous impact on human life. The best-known such revolution is the "Neolithic revolution" when man learned to domesticate plants and animals so that for the first time he had a measure of control over his food supply and was not dependent upon the bounty of nature. Such a step was a precondition to the development of cities or of any of the more elaborate manifesta-

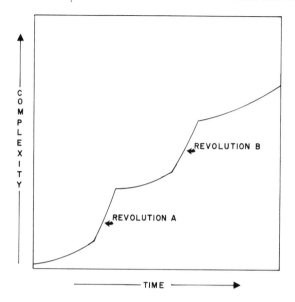

Fig. 99. The "revolutions" diagram of culture change. *Each "revolution" represents a time when major inventions or discoveries (such as agriculture) were altering man's life over a relatively short period. Such "revolutions" break the even tempo of gradual change and result in sharp upswings in cultural content and complexity.*

tions of civilizations; this point has been discussed in considering such finds as the Royal Cemetery at Ur. However, the "revolutions" interpretation also has flaws: First, the transition period is now known to span at least 2,000 years in both Old and New Worlds; "revolution" is not an accurate term to describe something that was a long and slow cultural transition. Second, there is also a question about where the "revolution" is placed in time. Should it be placed when the discovery is first made and the revolution is only potential? Or do we put it much later after a period of development when the major changes have actually come about?

Despite these problems, the diagram does introduce the conception that some "stages" are more important, more dramatic, or more drastic than others. It is useful, therefore, in its attempt to identify *important* changes.

3. *Cycles.* A third approach represents the "cyclical" or "decline and fall" school of thought, which sees culture change as a series of fluctuations, now advancing, now declining. This view of

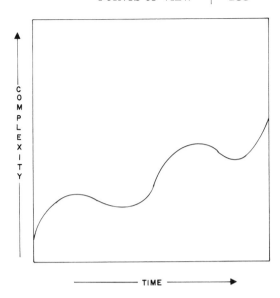

Fig. 100. The cyclical or "decline and fall" diagram of culture growth. *The lower parts of the curve represent "declines" or "dark ages" in which cultural knowledge is lost. The curve as a whole trends upward, however, since the rises have always been to levels of knowledge higher than any preceding.*

culture change indicates the existence of "dark ages" during which people lapse into a state of relative barbarism and lose many of the cultural features formerly possessed. Although a case can be made for such an explanation, a dark age in one aspect of culture (say politics or warfare) may be a time when some other feature (such as philosophy or technology) is flourishing. Hence, although it has some application to archaeological study, the cyclical diagram is less useful to the archaeologist than the other approaches. Its principal value is directing attention to the fact that change can be in both directions, regression as well as improvement.

4. *Complexity increase.* Culture change is often presented as a complexity curve, showing the rate at which culture changes through time. The extremes in rate of change can be seen by comparing man's first 300,000 years, in which the archaeologist can perceive only minimal changes in technology, with the last 100 years during which change has profoundly altered nearly every feature of human life. The complexity curve attempts to show that

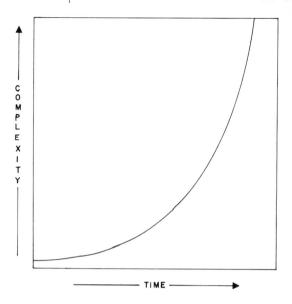

Fig. 101. A complexity curve. *The increasing steepness shows acceleration in cultural complexity and change. During the beginning period minimal increase in cultural content can be seen; in recent times many changes occur in very short time.*

there are more changes, closer together in time, as man's history goes on. Such a curve can be demonstrated for technological development as a whole, from the days of a few kinds of stone implements to the vast array of technological devices in use today. However, it does not seem applicable to technology for individual cultures and it has only doubtful application to nontechnological aspects of culture such as religion or social organization.

5. *Branching growth.* A final popular way of visualizing culture change is by reference to a "tree" diagram in which a simple and basic "trunk" is portrayed as branching out in many directions as a tree grows. Such a model shows both increasing diversity through time and continuity from one culture to its successor. Its main disadvantage is that it does not allow for interchange among the "branches." That is, it does not take into account the phenomenon of complex diffusion nor the many ways in which a culture can be influenced and changed by other contemporary cultures. A variation of the diagram views the tree as covered with "vines," crossing back and forth and connecting different "branches" with one

TIME

Fig. 102. The "tree" diagram of culture growth. *Each branch represents a new culture, originating from the "trunk" at a particular point in time and then developing in its own direction, giving rise in turn to other cultures. Cultures which become extinct are indicated by the branches which do not reach the top of the chart (the present).*

another. Unfortunately, a detailed presentation of this kind soon becomes so intricate that it loses the principal advantage of any diagram, namely the ordering of a large and complex structure into a readily understood pattern.

A variant form of this kind of diagram can be seen in a chart developed by R. J. Braidwood (Fig. 103). In this case, a three-dimensional effect is given the individual lines of development so that one can visualize the influence of one area on another and the geographic spread of cultural influences.

6. *Taxonomic diagram.* A somewhat different kind of diagram, not intended to show change but rather relationship among cultures, is a taxonomic chart on the so-called Midwestern or McKern system. This diagram, which has influenced American archaeologists, arranges cultures by analogy to the zoological classification

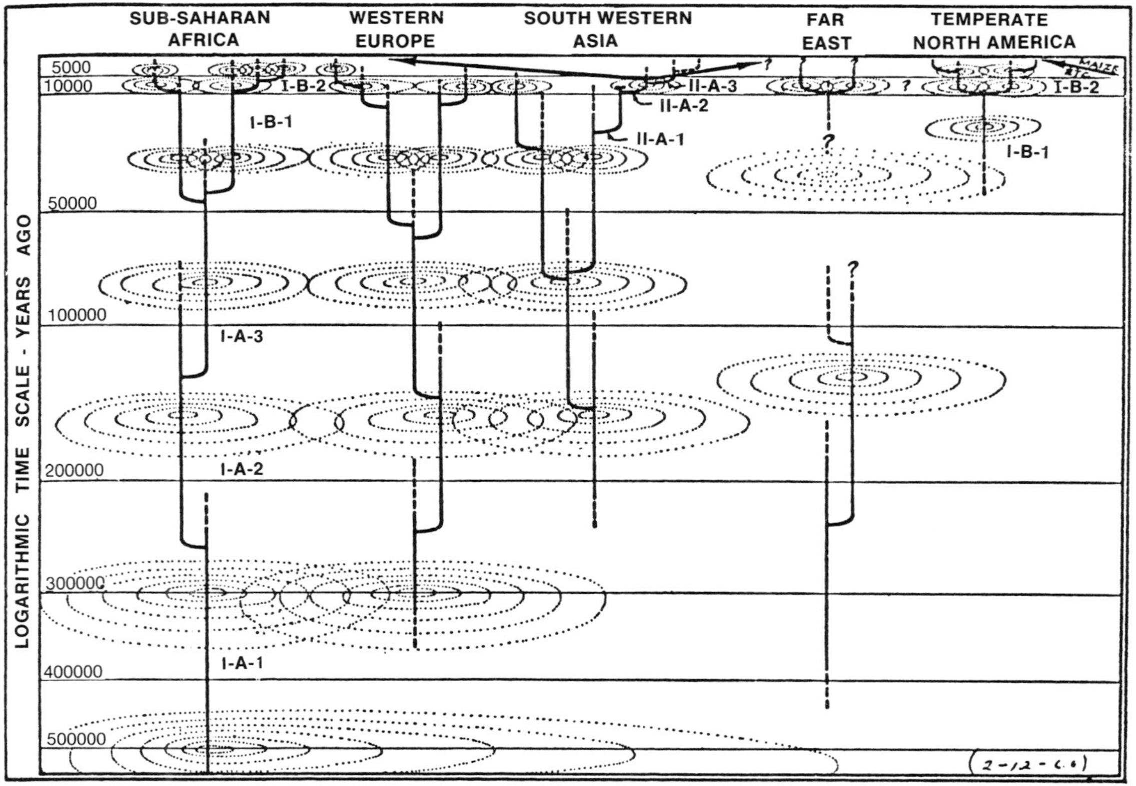

Fig. 103. Braidwood's diagram of culture-history developments. *This attempts to show space, time, and cultural connections, thereby combining several of the simpler diagrammatic ways of viewing culture history. Levels of time are shown, on which are simple "tree" diagrams showing the branching off of new cultures, with dotted lines indicating waves of influence from one area to another. A logarithmic time scale is used to allow for the accelerating rate of culture change. From "Levels in Prehistory: A Model for the Consideration of the Evidence" by R. J. Braidwood, Evolution After Darwin, University of Chicago Press, 1960. Reprinted by permission of the author and the University of Chicago Press. Copyright 1960 by the University of Chicago.*

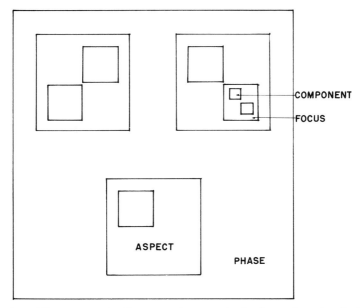

Fig. 104. The taxonomic diagram. *A way of viewing cultural relationships by analogy to zoological categories. The smallest cultural unit (the* com- ponent) *is the individual archaeological site; a* focus *is a group of closely related sites; an* aspect *may represent the culture of a whole state; and* phases *represent fundamental groupings of cultures on the basis of subsistence techniques within broad geographic regions. The taxonomic system provides a useful way of viewing relationships at a particular time, but it is difficult to use when there is much time depth to be considered since the pattern of similarities is apt to change markedly with time.*

system, starting with the smallest unit (the individual archaeological site) and continuing through larger and larger (and more and more general) cultural units. The system has advantages in showing degrees of relationship. However, as a scheme of classification it has gained limited acceptance because it does not readily lend itself to comparisons through time and is little applicable to the archaeologist's central concern: cultural change and development. With this pattern, one gains a picture of the relationships existing at a particular point in time; it is like using a large and detailed snapshot to understand a motion picture.

Archaeology is still in the stage of providing the descriptions necessary to test theoretical statements, and the general diagrams just given must be considered pioneering attempts to develop gen-

eral statements about culture change, with all the credit due pioneers and all the vulnerability to criticisms based on more
adequate descriptive data.

Except for the taxonomic diagram which shows relationships
at one point in time, the other views all show time as a major
dimension; the lack of time dimension is the chief criticism of
the taxonomic scheme. It is natural that the archaeologist should
be concerned with time — he cannot go beyond the descriptive
reconstruction of individual cultures until he can determine the
ages of his ancient cultures. Yet the dimension of time and the
measurement of culture change are not solely the concern of the
archaeologist and the historian — they are essential in many
kinds of social-science studies. Not all social scientists fully realize the fundamental part that studies of culture change play in
their individual researches, but the framework of culture change
can be seen in such fields as economics (business cycles), political
science ("controlled change"), history — necessarily, sociology
(various studies of population change, urbanism), and anthropology (not alone the archaeological part of it but all acculturation
studies and most ethnography). There are exceptions primarily
concerned with individual, rather than social, events (much of
psychology) and social-science studies which focus on the cultural behavior of a particular point in time (much sociology and
some anthropology). Yet even the exceptions often turn to change
through time when seeking explanations of general or universal
application.

Many studies of man can be done ignoring time, change, and
pattern. But the great adventure of archaeology is the search
for patterns and meanings in the mass of individual sites and
ancient objects reflecting man's activities. The total sweep of human development, over a half million years or more, provides
infinite examples of man's attempts to live with nature, with his
fellow man, and with himself. Out of this multitude of ancient
efforts, some successful and some failures, some brilliant and some
uninspired, can come one sort of understanding of the human race.
In contributing this perspective the archaeologist adds his bit to
the work of many scholars concerned with people, with what people are and why they behave as they do.

It is dubious that anything we know of the ancient Egyptians or
of Peking man will serve as a solution to any immediate problem.

But our awareness and appreciation of the past contribute to our own self-realization. Having looked, however briefly, at the step-by-step progression of mankind, we may have a better understanding of where we are and how we got here. Let us not minimize the value of this understanding when it comes to deciding where to go next.

GLOSSARY

ACCULTURATION The process by which one culture influences or alters another.

ARTIFACT Any object showing manufacture or use by humans.

ASSEMBLAGE *See* COMPLEX.

AUSTRALOPITHECINAE The zoological family containing several manlike primates such as *Australopithecus*, *Paranthropus*, and *Zinjanthropus*, all found in southern Africa at the beginning of the Pleistocene period. The name is derived from *austral* (southern) and *pithecus* (ape).

BRONZE AGE (1) That period in Old World archaeology between the introduction of bronze and the introduction of iron. (2) Generically, refers to those cultures in which nonferrous metallurgy flourishes, and agriculture and urban life have been developed.

C-14 *See* RADIOCARBON.

CARBON-14 *See* RADIOCARBON.

CHOPPER A crude stone tool made by striking a limited number of flakes from the edge of a cobble or fist-size rock to produce a coarse cutting edge.

COMPLEX As a noun in archaeological usage, refers to a pattern of artifact types, buildings, and the like that occur together. When the pattern includes only objects of small size such as tools, the term "assemblage" is probably preferable. "Complex" implies a culture in the archaeological sense; "assemblage," merely a collection of contemporaneous specimens.

CULTURE In anthropological usage, the way of life characteristic of a human group or society, including all aspects of human behavior (technology,

190

social customs, beliefs, traditions, and values). The term has broad and varied meaning for different scholars and many definitions and discussions are in print. In archaeological terminology, *culture* usually means a complex or assemblage of material objects representative of a particular people at a particular time, and whatever behavioral, social, or religious patterns can be inferred from these material remains. *See also* MATERIAL CULTURE.

DENDROCHRONOLOGY Tree-ring dating. Determining the age of wood samples by matching the pattern of tree rings against a master calendar showing fluctuations in ring width through time.

FLAKING A technique of shaping stone by chipping away flakes of the material. *Percussion flaking* is done by striking the stone to be chipped with another stone or bone. *Pressure flaking* is done by pressing a blunt-pointed tool of antler or bone against the edge to be worked. Flaking is feasible with materials that are glassy in nature and fracture evenly (such as obsidian or flint); it is not feasible with materials such as granite or sandstone which are in general amenable to grinding processes.

FLORESCENCE In archaeological terminology, the period of maximum elaboration of a culture, particularly in material aspects such as art and architecture.

HOMINID Manlike; belonging to the zoological family including modern and fossil forms of man.

LOWER PALEOLITHIC *See* PALEOLITHIC.

MARGINAL In anthropology, refers to traits or cultures which are either: (a) at a great distance from the center of development; or (b) simple in comparison to more complex developments elsewhere. The term is comparative and has no meaning except with reference to a specified center. Many examples are marginal in both senses.

MATERIAL CULTURE All objects manufactured or used by a particular human group. The distinction is made between those aspects of culture that appear as physical objects, and those aspects which are nonmaterial. "Religion" for example, as a system of beliefs and practices, need not appear as a part of material culture even though it is an essential part of all living cultures. In point of fact, there are usually many objects of material culture that are a reflection of religious beliefs and practices, temples, altars, idols, and standardized material symbols such as crosses.

MESOLITHIC (1) The Middle Stone Age in the Old World, representing the time between the extinction of many of the large game animals of the Pleistocene and the inception of the Neolithic (and agriculture). In western Europe, the Mesolithic began about 11,000 years ago. Mesolithic sites characteristically contain evidence for the use of small animals and shellfish as well as grinding implements for the preparation of plant foods. (2) Any culture regardless of age which shows the above adaptive pattern. In the New World, cultures of Mesolithic type appear at about the same time and apparently for the same reasons as in the Old World.

MIDDEN   The refuse accumulating as a result of the living activities of a group of people; an archaeological site composed of such refuse. The usual midden is a mound composed of ash, soil, and food remains like shells and animal bones. Sometimes the midden is a dump or trash pile separate from the residential area, but more commonly among hunters and gatherers the houses are on top of the midden itself. For this reason, middens also contain broken, lost, and discarded artifacts, cooking hearths, and often house remains and graves. A *shell midden* is a midden having as one of its principal components marine or fresh-water shells resulting from a shellfish-collecting economy.

NEOLITHIC   (1) The New Stone Age in the Old World, originally defined on the appearance of stone tools made by grinding and polishing. The significant markers for the beginning of the Neolithic are the introduction of agriculture, pottery, and sedentary farming communities. (2) Any culture regardless of age which practices systematic agriculture but lacks metallurgy.

OBSIDIAN   Volcanic glass. A favored material for primitive tool making, particularly after the advent of pressure-flaking techniques, because it can be easily chipped into precise and delicate forms.

OLDOWAN   The archaeological culture associated with the remains of the *Australopithecinae* and *Homo habilis*. The artifacts consist of very crude choppers and hammerstones; the name is derived from Olduvai Gorge in Tanganyika where the first specimens were identified.

PALEOLITHIC   (1) The Old Stone Age in the Old World, characterized by stone implements made exclusively by chipping techniques. (2) Any culture, regardless of age, which possesses only rough chipped-stone implements. In the Old World, the Lower Paleolithic lasts from the beginning of tool making until the inception of the various tool complexes of the Upper Paleolithic, about 40,000 years ago.

PERCUSSION FLAKING   *See* FLAKING.

PIT HOUSE   A semisubterranean house built over an excavated floor area, the floor level being from a few inches to several feet below the ground surface. A house type commonly used by hunter-gatherer peoples.

PLEISTOCENE   The geological period immediately preceding the Recent (which includes roughly the last 12,000 years). The Pleistocene lasted approximately one to two million years and was characterized by a series of climatic fluctuations resulting in: (a) glaciers widely spread in the northern hemisphere at different times; (b) major fluctuation in sea level as a result of the water frozen in, or melted from, the glaciers; (c) the spread of a mammalian fauna including many large forms (mammoth, giant bison, and other) which became extinct at the beginning of the Recent period.

PLIOCENE   Geological period preceding the Pleistocene.

POTASSIUM-ARGON   A dating technique relying on the relative amount of radioactive isotopes of potassium and argon in rocks. Used for long-range dating; not applicable to time ranges of a few thousand years.

PRESSURE FLAKING   *See* FLAKING.

PRIMATE   Member of the order of mammals that includes monkeys, apes, and men.

RADIOCARBON   Dating technique depending upon the constant decay rate of C-14 in organic materials such as wood, charcoal, or shell. The half-life of C-14 was originally determined as 5570 ± 30 years, meaning that half of the original C-14 in the sample will disintegrate in that time. Recent studies of the decay rate indicate the half-life to be 5730 ± 40 years, which would make the published radiocarbon dates too young by about 3 per cent.

SHELL MIDDEN   *See* MIDDEN.

SHERD   A fragment of pottery. A variant is *shard*, not used in archaeological writing.

SITE   In archaeological usage, any location showing evidence of previous human occupation, including such things as quarries, paintings on rocks, temporary camps, middens, and cities.

STAGE   A technological level of development, with its accompanying social and religious features.

TECHNOLOGY   Industrial science; tools and their application.

TRADITION   In archaeological usage, the persistence of particular tool types or assemblages over a long period of time in a given region. Examples: the chopping-tool tradition of South Asia; the fist-ax tradition of Europe.

UPPER PALEOLITHIC   *See* PALEOLITHIC.

INDEX